CALLED TO BATTLE, DESTINED TO WIN

One of the greatest joys of my life and ministry has been my up-close, personal and covenant relationship with Jerry and Carolyn Savelle. For 40 years I have watched them walk in love, by faith, from victory to victory in integrity before the Lord Jesus Christ. They have been a great inspiration and blessing to my life.

KENNETH COPELAND

Founder of Kenneth Copeland Ministries, Fort Worth, Texas

When I think of Jerry Savelle, I think of integrity, I think of honor, and I think of loyalty. God truly has blessed this generation with a man who has not only touched the world for the Lord Jesus Christ but also touched the hearts of many people—including mine! You won't find a finer man than Jerry Savelle.

JESSE DUPLANTIS

Founder of Jesse Duplantis Ministries, Destrehan, Lousiana

I congratulate my dear friend Jerry Savelle on 40 years in the ministry. I salute you, honor you and cherish your friendship. Called to Battle, Destined to Win will bless multitudes.

DODIE OSTEEN

Cofounder of Lakewood Church, Houston, Texas

Jerry Savelle is always anointed. He is always prepared by the Holy Spirit, and he gets the job done. I rank Jerry with Stephen in the Bible and admire him with all my heart!

ORAL ROBERTS

Founder of Oral Roberts Evangelistic Association
Founder of Oral Roberts University, Tulsa, Oklahoma

CALLED TO
BATTLE
DESTINED TO
WIN

Experience God's Breakthrough Power in Your Life

JERRY SAVELLE

Regal

From Gospel Light
Ventura, California, U.S.A.

Published by Regal
From Gospel Light
Ventura, California, U.S.A.
www.regalbooks.com
Printed in the U.S.A.

Library of Congress Cataloging-in-Publication Data
Savelle, Jerry.
Called to battle, destined to win / Jerry Savelle.
p. cm.
ISBN 978-0-8307-4805-1 (hard cover) —
ISBN 978-0-8307-5129-7 (international trade paper)
1. Success—Religious aspects—Christianity. 2. Christian life.
3. Vocation—Christianity. I. Title.
BV4598.3.S28 2009
248.4—dc22
2008047992

1 2 3 4 5 6 7 8 9 10 11 12 13 14 15 / 15 14 13 12 11 10 09

Rights for publishing this book outside the U.S.A. or in non-English languages are
administered by Gospel Light Worldwide, an international not-for-profit ministry.
For additional information, please visit www.glww.org, email info@glww.org, or write to
Gospel Light Worldwide, 1957 Eastman Avenue, Ventura, CA 93003, U.S.A.

CONTENTS

CHAPTER 1

MAKING CHAMPIONS
OUT OF NOBODIES

Born to Be a Champion

If you've ever been called a nobody, then you qualify to become a champion. God is a master at making champions. If God can do what He did with Saul of Tarsus, He can do the same for you. If He can do what He did with Simon Bar-Jona, He can do the same for you. If He can do what He did with me, He can do the same for you.

I was once a nobody. I was insignificant. But God found this nobody in an auto body shop in Shreveport, Louisiana, and said, "You know what? I believe I can use that nobody!" I asked Him, "Do You have any idea what You are getting when You get me?" God told me, "Don't worry about it. I am a master at making champions out of nobodies!"

Jeremiah 29:11 tells us, " 'For I know the plans I have for you,' says the LORD. 'They are plans for good and not for disaster, to give you a future and a hope' " (*NLT*). God doesn't have one evil thought in His mind about you. He is not planning disaster or destruction for your life. Some folks have the idea that God sits around thinking up ways that He can wreak havoc on their life just to teach them something. But that's not what He does. God thinks thoughts of peace about you to "give you hope in your final outcome" (Jer. 29:11, *AMP*). The passage in Jeremiah continues, " 'In those days when you pray, I will listen. If you look for me in earnest, you will find me when you seek me. I will be found by you,' says the LORD. 'I will end your captivity and restore your fortunes' " (Jer. 29:12-13, *NLT*).

Failure is not in God's plan for any of His children. His desire is that you thrive in every endeavor in life. God wants you to succeed. He wants you to live in divine health. He wants you to be prosperous. I thank God for men like brother Oral Roberts, who let us know many years ago that God is a good God. Brother Roberts began preaching a number of years ago from the third book of John, "Beloved, I pray that you may prosper in every way and [that your body] may keep well, even as [I know] your soul keeps well and prospers" (3 John 1:2, *AMP*).

I think about half the church world fought him over it. Many people didn't think it was God's will that we live in health or that we live prosperously. God bless the pioneers who kept on preaching this message regardless of public opinion. Thank God that many of us today hold strong to that revelation.

Failure is not in God's plan for any of His children. His desire is that you thrive in every endeavor in life.

Someone once asked the well-known entrepreneur J. C. Penney, "What would you say is the key or the secret to your success?" He answered, "Adversity. I've always faced adversity, but it has brought something out of me and made me a success." If that's what it takes to live a successful life, then you and I have got what it takes, because we have an adversary who is persistent in his attempts to kill us, steal from us and destroy us. That doesn't mean we have to lie down, roll over, play dead and let him do with us what he will. Satan seeks whomever he may devour, but you can tell him, "You may not devour me!"

I'm sure you have had your share of adversity, and I know you'll continue to have more, but these challenges have a way of bringing out the champion on the inside of you. When you were born again, you were born to be a champion. You were born to be a winner. You are not a loser, so don't call yourself a loser and don't allow anyone else to convince you that you are a loser.

I realize that one of the greatest battles people fight is with words that have been spoken over them. I've heard many people speak negative words over others. It grieves my spirit when I hear a parent call his or her little child "stupid" or say things like, "You will never amount to anything. You were born poor and you'll always be poor." You may have had such "curses" spoken over you, and I know it's hard for you to overcome those things. But be encouraged, because you can overcome them. The Word of God is more powerful than anything someone says. There is no weapon formed against you that will prosper (see Isa. 54:17).

God has planned a bright future for you. Before He ever flung the stars into space, He had already planned your life. He knows how it's going to turn out, but it's up to you to get into the flow of what God designed for you. Our lives need to match His plan.

God Wants You to Be Blessed!

The book of Psalms tells us that God is "mindful of us" (Ps. 115:12, *KJV*). He's got us on His mind. But what exactly is He thinking about? This verse goes on to say, "He will bless us." Now that should answer the question of what God thinks about when He thinks about you. God wonders, *How can I bless my people?*

How can I get them in a position to experience my blessings? God's not trying to keep things from us. He's doing His best to get good things to us. Because God orders the steps of good men and women, He is always endeavoring to get us into a position to receive. If we will listen to Him, then we will always be in the right place at the right time and become the recipients of His blessing. That's why we need to be sensitive to His leadership.

There are miracles out there that belong to you. There are blessings out there that belong to you. There is financial prosperity out there that belongs to you. "He [God] will bless them that fear the LORD, both small and great. The LORD shall increase you more and more" (Ps. 115:13-14, *KJV*). The most natural thing for you to experience as a child of God is increase in every area of your life—your spirit, soul, mind, body and finances. All areas. God has no problem with you increasing more and more.

The secular world, however, has a problem with us increasing, and carnal-minded Christians have a problem with you and me increasing. But God has no problem with it. He really doesn't care how many banks it takes to hold all your increase. The only thing He's concerned about is how you handle the increase and that you honor Him with it. Remember, it is God who gives us "power to get wealth" (Deut. 8:18, *KJV*).

I remember a few years ago when brother Roberts was involved in a particular project and I sent him an offering that I considered to be a sizable seed back then. I received a handwritten letter from him that said: "Dear Jerry, Evelyn and I appreciate you and your family and your daughters. We appreciate your partnership in this ministry. . . . I'm believing for you for a thousandfold return on your gift!"

A thousandfold! I've had days when I was happy if God would match me dollar for dollar. Haven't you? I used to think, *God, I'm not even going to be concerned about thirtyfold, just with what I've sown. That will meet my need today.* We can't think like that. We have to enlarge our vision.

The Bible tells us that obedience is definitely a key to the miraculous. God told Job, "If they obey and serve [Me], they shall spend their days in prosperity, and their years in pleasures" (Job 36:11, *KJV*). A few years ago the Spirit of God said this to me: "Many of My people go around confessing and believing that Abraham's blessings are theirs. Well, if they're going to believe for the blessings of Abraham, then they must accept the call of Abraham." Do you know what the call of Abraham was? To bless the families of the earth. This is especially why God has no problem with you increasing and being blessed.

The word "blessed" means empowered to prosper. God wants you to prosper. But if you're going to lay hold of that, then you must also use it for the reason for which God is giving it to you— to be a blessing. The greatest joy you'll ever know in your life is when you are a blessing. I also like to define blessing as the ability to prevent misfortune in the lives of others. If somebody can't pay his rent, and you're blessed, then you can prevent misfortune in his life by paying his rent. If a family's old car is worn out, and you're blessed, then you can prevent misfortune in their life by buying them a new car. I found out that if you stop being a blessing, then you will cut off the blessings in your own life. So don't abuse or misuse prosperity. Believe God for it, and then use it for the reason God gave it to you.

The moment you begin to seek God with all your heart, He will begin the process of turning your life around.

God has always intended for us to live a blessed and prosperous life. He's got some extremely exciting things on the horizon for you and me. Our future is bright; and according to the verses that we read in Jeremiah, God wants us to be filled with hope regarding our final outcome. No matter how miserable your life may be at this very moment, God's plan is to turn it around. He said that if you won't run from Him but turn to Him when you're distressed, He will bring you out of captivity. The moment you begin to seek Him with all your heart, He will begin the process of turning your life around.

"I [God] will answer them before they even call to me. While they are still talking about their needs, I will go ahead and answer their prayers!" (Isa. 65:24, *NLT*). God is declaring that before you even utter the very first word of your prayer, He's already preparing a solution or a way out of your circumstances. While you are still calling on Him, He's already involved in dispatching His angels to go forth and change your circumstances. Why? Because it's never God's will that you fail. It's never God's will that you stay in captivity. It's never God's will that you stay in bondage.

The miracle you need, the manifestation you are believing for and the answer you've been praying for could come to pass even before you finish reading this book!

Forget About What Others Think or Say; It's God that Matters

God intends for you to be a winner, not a loser. "Now thanks be unto God, who always causeth us to triumph in Christ" (2 Cor. 2:14, *KJV*). God's will is that we *always* win! Don't ever give up until you triumph. I don't care if you fall and stumble 10 times. Get up and go again! You don't get 3 strikes in this game. You get as many pitches as it takes to knock it out of the park.

You have the blood of Jesus running through your veins. You are a born winner. You are a champion on the inside. And it's time the devil begins to see that champion arise on the outside. Your background has nothing to do with whether or not you qualify to be a champion in life. Your past failures have nothing to do with it. Your past mistakes have nothing to do with it. You need to always put your confidence and trust in God's ability to make you a champion.

Paul wrote, "Remember, dear brothers and sisters, that few of you were wise in the world's eyes, or powerful, or wealthy when God called you. Instead, God deliberately chose things the world considers foolish in order to shame those who think they are wise. And he chose things that are powerless to shame those who are powerful. God chose things despised by the world, things counted as nothing at all, and used them to bring to nothing what the world considers important, so that no one can ever boast in the presence of God" (1 Cor. 1:26-29, *NLT*).

God is not necessarily looking for people who have impressive credentials or the right education as far as the world is concerned to qualify to be a champion. There's nothing wrong with credentials or education, but God doesn't really care if you are an expert in those areas. He is saying that whomever the world says can't be used, He can use. If the world says there is absolutely no hope for you, God says you are a candidate for His use. If your parents, your relatives, your friends or your coworkers think that you will never amount to anything, just remember that God says you can amount to something. All nobodies qualify.

I believe God is looking for a group of winners to rise up today and show the world that the God you and I serve is far greater than the image that stuffy religion portrays of Him. For the most part, the world thinks that Christians are a bunch of weaklings, misfits and castaways who are useless to society. But we are changing the image of Christianity. We are not losers; we are winners. We are not failures; we are champions! On the inside of you is unlimited potential. *God has chosen you.*

When I think of my friend evangelist Dennis Burke, one of the greatest teachers in the Body of Christ today, I appreciate the anointing of God on his life. But would you believe that he used to be a long-haired, drug-addicted hippie who doesn't even remember high school because he was in some other world while it was going on? If he had never shared that testimony, I wouldn't have believed it myself.

I think about Pastor Happy Caldwell. This man, who pastors one of the greatest churches in America today and pioneered the very first Christian television network in the state of Arkansas, used to be a nobody. He used to be a liquor salesman. And look at him now. Brother Caldwell has come a long way.

If the world says there is absolutely no hope for you, God says you are a candidate for His use. All nobodies qualify.

I think about another preacher, Jesse Duplantis. God made a champion out of a rock-'n'-roller-heathen-from-hell. And I also think about brother Oral Roberts who as a young boy was ashamed of his stuttering problem and believed he would never amount to anything. No one else did either. Satan had marked him to destroy his life, but God looked at this nobody and turned him into a champion. Brother Roberts has accomplished so much in his life and has brought much healing to his generation.

It's time for you to get over your past. It's time for you to get over what everybody thinks of you. It's time for you to get over all the negative words that have been spoken over you. It's time for you to get over all your previous mistakes. It's time for you to get over all your failures. God says He can use you. He needs you. He wants you. He desires to turn you into a champion.

There are plenty of people in the Bible who, in the eyes of others, were considered nobodies that God used to change the world. A story is told in 1 Samuel about a boy named David. God had instructed the prophet Samuel to go and anoint the next king of Israel. Samuel went to the house of a man named Jesse and told him to bring out all of his sons to let him look at them. God told Samuel that one of them would be the next king. Jesse brought them out one by one except for the youngest son. The insignificant one. A simple sheepherder. But God told Samuel, "Don't judge by his appearance. . . . The LORD doesn't make decisions the way you do! People judge by outward appearance, but the LORD looks at a person's thoughts and intentions" (1 Sam. 16:7, *NLT*). I am so thankful for that.

After I accepted the call to the ministry, I came to Fort Worth to hear brother Kenneth Copeland preach at a church called Grace Temple. My wife, Carolyn, and I were just starting to prepare ourselves for the ministry. We went over there in an old dogged car that had over 100,000 miles on it. We barely had enough money to get to that meeting. Once we arrived, I stopped by brother Copeland's office and he happened to be there. At the time, he had maybe three employees. I walked right in and announced that I had shut down my business and was going into full-time ministry. Later, he told me that he immediately thought to himself, *Oh, God! Jerry's not ready for this.* He even once publicly said that he thought I had the anointing of a duck, and probably couldn't preach my way out of a wet paper bag. Well, the Spirit of God spoke to him and said, *Don't look on the outward appearance.*

God looks at what's on the inside. Men look at the outward appearance. They'll tell you that you don't qualify, that you'll never make it, that nothing good could happen to you. But you can't go by what others say. It's not others who are responsible for your calling. It's God. It's not others who determine whether you are anointed of God or not. It's God. It's not others who will make you successful. It's God.

Getting back to Samuel, after looking at all of Jesse's sons and knowing not one of them was right for the job, he asked Jesse if he had any more boys. In *THE MESSAGE* translation, Jesse responded, "Well, yes, there's the runt. But he's out tending the sheep" (1 Sam. 16:11). Boy, be very careful when you run into "runts." When people start talking about other folks like they are nobodies, watch those nobodies very closely. They're liable to turn into champions. When Jesse brought David in, you can imagine what he must have looked and smelled like after tending the sheep. He looked nothing like a king. But what happened? "So as David stood there among his brothers, Samuel took the olive oil he had brought and poured it on David's head. And the Spirit of the LORD came mightily upon him from that day on" (1 Sam. 16:13, *NLT*).

Samuel didn't anoint David privately. He did it in front of all the others who qualified in the natural. He did it in front of all those who surely thought they would have been chosen. In the eyes of men, David was the least likely to be the next king; but not in the eyes of God.

So what if others can't see in you what God sees? So what if your family doesn't think what you are believing for can happen to you? So what if your friends laugh and persecute you? So what if there's never been any indication in your life that you are a potential champion? So what if you've failed at everything you've ever attempted in days past. If God says you are a champion, then you are a champion. If God says you can do it, then you can do it. If God says you are, then you are.

Champions Are Not Created Overnight

There's something very important about this story in 1 Samuel. Even though Samuel anointed David to be king when he was a young boy, it didn't happen overnight. In fact, as soon as the ceremony was over, David went right back to what he was doing, herding sheep. Even though you find out today that God sees you as a champion, don't become discouraged because you don't turn into one by tomorrow. You will probably go back to doing whatever you were doing—working in that office, that shop or that place of business—and others may not be able to see any change at all.

While David was anointed king and still tending his father's flocks, his brothers mocked him. "So, you're the king, huh? What are you the king of? A bunch of sheep?" There are a lot of folks out there who won't see what you see. You need to learn not to be moved by what you see, what you hear and what you feel. Some of my relatives thought I'd lost my mind when they found out I was going to be a preacher. But now when they are in some kind of need they call the boy they once thought had lost his mind. Why? Because that little nobody has become a champion.

If you read the rest of the story, the leader of Israel, King Saul, finally called for David's help and found him right where the prophet Samuel found him the first time, in the fields with the sheep. But David wasn't discouraged. He had stayed faithful to the calling of God on his life.

Don't give up. Don't be discouraged.
Don't quit. God is still working in your life even though
you may feel nothing is coming to pass.

You must stay faithful to God and His Word and not allow others to distract or discourage you. Today you may be in debt up to your eyeballs. You may be the most miserable person around. You might not be able to remember the last time you succeeded at anything. But on the inside of you there is a champion that is ready to come out, a champion that is ready to be born into this earth. So don't give up. Don't be discouraged. Don't quit. God is still working in your life even though you may feel nothing is coming to pass.

Brother Kenneth Copeland and his wife, Gloria, started out as nobodies. Just over 43 ago they were boiling potatoes in a coffee pot because they had no stove. They were so deep in debt that they could hardly see straight. It didn't take 40 years, however, for them to accomplish what they have achieved through that time. God was working the entire time. There are no shortcuts to victory. You are going to have to keep standing on the Word of God, just like all the other champions, but also understand that

God is accelerating things. In the meantime, you must stand. You must persevere. You must be uncompromising.

Goliath and the Road to Victory

The true test of David's faithfulness was when he faced the giant Goliath. Goliath represented David's first major obstacle that attempted to keep him from becoming what God said he was to become. Goliath, like our adversary Satan, stood between David and his destiny. Satan will create all sorts of barriers, obstacles, tests and trials, because he knows that God has a wonderful future planned for you; so Satan wants you to become discouraged and quit. I want you to understand that even though Goliath symbolized David's first major roadblock, David chose to make Goliath a stepping-stone instead of a stumbling block.

I like what I heard Jesse Duplantis say one time. He and I were tag-team preaching together about David. I'd say something about the story and then Jesse would take it over from there. In our message, I'd gotten to the point where David had cut off Goliath's head and was carrying it around as a trophy. I tagged Jesse to take over, and his opening remark was, "What God was trying to show David was how to get 'a-head' in life. Most people think God made David a king, but Goliath made David a king!"

The very thing that was standing between David and his future was what God used to make him a great leader. The adversity you're experiencing today, the thing that is trying to keep you from your destiny, could become a stepping-stone to your greatest victory. In other words, you can turn every test into a testimony.

Champions Attract Nobodies

David not only became a champion, but he also had this unique ability to turn other nobodies into champions. I remember hearing brother Oral Roberts talk about how his ministry attracted nobodies as far as the religious world was concerned. He attracted the unlearned, the ignorant, the nobodies. But those unlearned, ignorant nobodies built a famous university that has been led and inspired by the Holy Spirit for many years. After a while, when other folks who once saw you as a nobody now recognize you as a champion, they suddenly want to be around you. They start to believe that if God can turn your life around, then He can do it for them as well.

Let's look at the kind of people David attracted. "David therefore departed, and escaped to the cave Adullam: and when his brethren and all his father's house heard it, they went down thither to him. And every one that was in distress, and every one that was in debt, and every one that was discontented, gathered themselves unto him; and he became a captain over them: and there were with him about four hundred men" (1 Sam. 22:1-2, *KJV*).

What in the world are you going to accomplish with 400 people who are in distress, in debt and discontented? If you study this passage, however, you'll find out that this same group of people became the mighty men of David. I talk about some of them in chapter 2. These were the mightiest warriors in all of Israel, but they were nobodies when David first met them.

The word "distressed" in the Hebrew language is literally translated as "under great pressure or stress." You may be reading this book today while under great pressure and great stress. But I've got a good report for you. If you feel under heavy pressure, you are in the right place. You are in the place to become a champion. Have you got so many debts that there is absolutely no way to pay them all off? Then you are in the right place to become a champion. Are you discontented? Do you feel wounded in your spirit and your soul? Do you feel rejected and ridiculed? Then you are in the right place to become a champion!

Pastor Creflo Dollar's beginning days were full of debt, distress and discontent. His congregation at first was a bunch of wounded people with debt up to their eyeballs. But down on the inside of Creflo and all the men and women who were part of his church were champions.

You might be thinking, *I hear what you're saying, brother Jerry, but you don't understand my past.* I say, "Get over it!" You might be thinking, *But you don't understand where I come from.* I say, "Get over it!" You might be thinking, *You don't understand the mistakes I've made.* I say, "Get over it!" You might be thinking, *I've never amounted to anything.* I say, "Get over it!" You are a champion; and it's time you start forgetting about everything behind you and start watching as God turns you into a champion who can change the world.

2

CALLED TO BATTLE

No Exceptions: God Wants You in His Army

We are called to battle. This is not an option; it is a command. The apostle Paul tells us that we are "called" or, as I like to say, summoned: "Fight the good fight of faith, lay hold on eternal life, whereunto thou art also called, and hast professed a good profession before many witness" (1 Tim. 6:12, *KJV*). When a person is "called" of God, that means God has summoned him or her. If you get a speeding ticket and are summoned to appear in court, you are required to show up. Sure, you can ignore it if you want. You can crumple it up and toss the summons in the trash, but I'll tell you what, the law will catch up with you sooner or later.

When God calls someone into the ministry, He summons him or her. I first heard that call in 1957, when I was 11 years old. I was visiting my grandmother in Oklahoma City, and I heard brother Roberts preaching as I watched on an old black-and-white television. I had never heard of him and knew absolutely nothing about him. My relatives, though, because they lived in Oklahoma, were very familiar with his ministry. Brother Roberts was preaching one of his most famous tent meeting sermons, and I was captivated by it. At that moment, I felt called by God to preach the gospel.

I'll be honest. Preaching was the last thing on my mind when I was 11 years old. When I was 9, I had already determined what I was going to do with my life. I was going to be just like my daddy, who was in the automotive business. When it came to cars, you name it and he did it. He repaired wrecked cars, built hot rods, and customized and raced them. I just knew, even as a 9-year-old kid, that one day my life was going to be centered around automobiles, especially around a racetrack. Every weekend my dad and I were at some racetrack. He raced everything—sports cars, sprint cars, stock cars, modified hot rods. I wanted him to teach me the trade and I wanted to know everything he knew. I, too, was going to build, fix, customize and race cars. Nothing and nobody could stop me from believing in this dream. Nobody but God, that is. He had different ideas. He had summoned me.

When you are 11 years old and have already figured out what you're going to do with your life, and God shows up interfering with all your plans, you get a little upset. So here's what I planned. I just thought to myself, *Well, if I never tell anyone about this experience, then I won't have to do it. God will realize that He made a mistake and He will choose somebody else.* So I kept my mouth shut and never said a word about it to anybody. I just got real busy pursuing what I wanted to do and just assumed I'd never have to do this preaching stuff. I ignored my God-given summons.

By 1966, when Carolyn and I married, I was working at automotive dealerships and endeavoring to make enough money to go into business for myself. Two years later, I owned my own shop and was doing exactly what I said I would do. But God hadn't given up on me just yet. You see, Carolyn was a filled-with-the-Spirit believer, and the night before we got married she told me, "I just want you to know I made a vow to God when I was eight years old. I promised Him that the man I marry will be born again, filled with the Holy Spirit, preach the gospel and go to Africa." I just about burst out laughing and said, "Honey, then you are marrying the wrong man! I'm not doing any of those things. I am going to race automobiles. And if you are going to marry me, then you are going to spend the rest of your life on a racetrack."

Carolyn didn't back down. She said, "You don't know the power of prayer." My blood was practically boiling at this point, and I told her, "Baby, you don't know how determined I am." "Don't worry," my beautiful wife assured me, "I can pray all of that out of you!"

I was living the American dream.
So why was I so miserable? Because I had received
a call from God I had purposely ignored.

Guess what? She was right. You don't see me in or hear my name announced at NASCAR or at Indy 500 events, do you? No! Why? Carolyn prayed it out of me! I'm telling you, this woman knows how to pray. The truth is, she prayed a lot of other stuff out of me too, but I won't get into that right now. Believe me, I know there are many wives out there who have prayed many things out of their husbands!

In 1969, I could not run from this call anymore, even though I was doing what I had dreamed of doing as a young boy. I should have been the happiest person on the planet. I was married. I had two daughters. I owned my own business. I had a new home. I was living the American dream. But you know what? The truth was that on the inside I was miserable. Sounds ridiculous, doesn't it? But it wasn't. Why was I so miserable? Because I had received a call from God that I had purposely ignored.

The Bible says that the callings of God are without repentance (see Rom. 11:29). What that means is this: I could have lived and died not preaching the gospel, but when I got to heaven, God would judge me according to my calling. He wouldn't ask me, "So, Jerry, how did you do at Indy?" or "So, Jerry, how did you do on the racetrack?" No. God would say, "So, Jerry, what did you do with that call on your life?" The callings of God are without repentance.

That year, I finally surrendered my life to God's call and, as it was (and still is) in my nature, I went all-out for God 200 percent. I was never able to do anything halfway, and following the Lord's command was no exception. As we say in Texas, I went whole hog. I gave it my all. Now God did not destroy my passion for automobiles, particularly for the fast kinds. He has given me my dream back and turned even that into a ministry. Our organization created a Christian motorcycle outreach called Chariots of Light and Christian Car Club, and we are invading car and motorcycle shows all around the country. I also happen to own some very, very nice classic automobiles. In fact, often I win "Best in Show" with my '57 Chevy Bellaire Convertible. Not only can I still compete with the best of them, but whenever we win, I have an opportunity to preach God's Word. He has turned everything I was passionate about before I surrendered my life to Him into an evangelistic outreach. Praise God!

You have a calling on your life. It may be to raise your children in a loving, peaceful environment—so teach them the Word of God by example. Your calling may be as a business owner, a manager or a supervisor, and God wants you to finance the gospel. You have a calling by God. It's not too late—too much time hasn't passed. You haven't blown it. You have a calling to fulfill.

It's a very serious thing to be called of God. Our lives are not just about playing church. I know that in some circles today it is a very popular thing to be involved in ministry, because it may look glamorous and can make you feel like someone important; but that is not the case. The call of God involves warfare.

All I am saying relates to what Paul said about fighting the good fight of faith. Notice he used the words "whereunto also ye were called." As I've said before, this fight is more than just a command; it's a call. God has *called you* to fight the good fight of faith. You do not have the right to run from battle. You do not have the right to give up. You do not have the right to quit. You do not have the right to throw in the towel. And you do not have the right to allow the devil to defeat you.

I realize many Christians want a comfortable Christianity. It's so easy to serve God when things are going smoothly. Just about anybody can raise their hands and shout, "Hallelujah!" But boy, oh boy, you just watch what happens to many believers the first time adversity rears its ugly head. They want to run. They want to hide. They want to do anything but stand and fight. The one thing I learned many years ago is that if you are not experiencing opposition from the adversary, you are apparently not much of a threat. You must already be compromising in some way because everybody that I know who believes God, stands on His Word and lives by faith inevitably comes under attack in some way, shape or form. When I preached this message once, some fellow came up to me and asked, "Should I believe for more attacks?" My answer was, "No. Just get serious with God and get into His Word. You will have all the attacks you can handle, but at the same time, get ready to walk in the greatest victories you have ever known."

**God has called you to fight the good fight of faith.
You do not have the right to run from the battle.**

In 1967, I received a letter from the United States government that began with the word "greetings." They decided they needed me to serve my country during the Vietnam War. I wound up at Fort Dix, New Jersey, for basic training. After those eight grueling weeks were over, I spent another eight weeks in AIT (Advanced Individual Training). Later I went to Fort Polk in Louisiana. If you went to Fort Polk in the 1960s, you knew your next stop was Vietnam. The southern part of that state is famous for its rice fields and was the closest replica of Vietnam. It was the perfect place to train.

But I had a praying wife. Matter of fact, Carolyn was praying like crazy. Our first daughter was born when I was in basic training, and she was three-and-a-half months old before I ever saw her. My wife, under no circumstances, was going to let me spend more time away from my family. But you know what? I was summoned by the government to serve my country and had to do whatever they asked of me. Uncle Sam sent me a letter that could not just be thrown away. Can you guess what happened? Carolyn's prayers worked! I wound up staying stateside and never went to Vietnam.

Quitting Is Not an Option

I like what brother Kenneth Copeland said more than 30 years ago: "The good fight of faith is the fight that you win." As we fight the good fight of faith, we are winning! This means we need to get the word "quit" out of our vocabulary. For those of you who have ever been to boot camp, you know very well the temptation to quit. When I arrived at Fort Dix, I was in for the shock of my life. Here I was, this good ol' Southern boy who didn't even know New Jersey existed. So when I got there, I was blown away. New Jerseyans talked so different that I couldn't understand what they were saying.

I arrived at the barracks on a bus with a group of young men, and there a drill sergeant who looked like Smokey the Bear greeted us. He started screaming and cussing and calling us every name in the book. Every name, that is, except our real names. I wasn't whatever filth he was calling me, so I waited until I heard him say "Jerry." He never did. This man got me out of the bus so fast that I never even knew what hit me.

He told our group to line up, and when we did, I looked around at this ragtag, motley crew of young men. On one end there was a guy in a three-piece suit; on the other end there was a Gomer Pyle look-alike wearing overalls; and standing right beside me in the middle was a hippie with hair as long in the front as it was in the back. I'll never forget that guy. He had on these bright green-and-white striped, bell-bottomed, hip-hugger pants with flowers sown everywhere. The man was so stoned he didn't even know he was there yet. The drill sergeant put his nose right on that hippie's nose and started yelling at him. "You filthy, sorry excuse for a human being. I'm gonna be your father, your mother, your brother and your granddaddy. I'm gonna make a man out of you. I'm gonna make a soldier out of you." Finally the hippie came out of his drug-induced comatose state, smiled without a care in the world and said, "Peace, brother, peace."

I started looking up and down that line of men and thought, *Is this all we have to work with? Are we going to war with this pathetic bunch? Dear God, help us!* But once I got involved in the basic training process, I quickly found out how serious the military leaders were about getting us prepared for war. They rode us. They harassed us. They beat us into physical and mental shape. The minute we were allowed to rest in our barracks, they came back and started all over again. You know, all of us were wondering, *What on earth did we do to deserve this kind of treatment?* It was so bad that we wanted to write letters to our mothers asking them to tell our congressmen how badly we were being treated. Some of the guys in our company couldn't take it, so they went AWOL. I will never forget what it was like seeing them get caught. The sergeants slapped handcuffs on them and marched them past the rest of us. The message was clear. "You have been summoned and you will do this thing whether you like it or not."

Thank God He does not have to put us in handcuffs. Still, I've noticed that many of us don't take the fight of faith as seriously as He does. You see, God does not intend to lose. He is going to get this job done, whatever it takes. When I looked at the line of men at basic training, I felt sorry for the U.S. government because we were all they had to work with. After I became a Christian, I started looking up and down the line of all the other believers, and I started feeling sorry for God. But we're growing, we're learning, we're being trained for battle and we're different now than we were before.

We have been called to battle. We have been called to fight. We have not been called to crack under pressure and give up. We are told in 2 Corinthians 2:14, "Now thanks be to God who always leads us in triumph in Christ" (*NKJV*). When I read that, here is what I get out of it: We are *destined* to win! In the mind of God, we are called to battle, but we are destined to win. The battle is not over until you triumph. God doesn't have the "win a few, lose a few" mentality. In God's mind, it's about winning them all. He has destined us to win all of our fights!

We have been called to battle. We have been called to fight. We have not been called to crack under pressure and give up.

God tells us to "triumph always." If we're honest with each other, we've all experienced setbacks at some time or another. I know I have. There have been times when I felt like a failure. There have been times when it looked like defeat was inescapable. There have been times when I've wanted to give up. But I've stamped that verse on my heart and determined a long time ago that even though I may get knocked down from time to time, and even though it may look like losing is unavoidable, the battle is not over until I triumph. I have been destined to win.

Our problem is that we give up too quickly. I am a boxing enthusiast. I don't know a gentle way to say this, but never sit in the same room with me when boxing is on TV, because I will literally hurt you! My wife and daughters have gotten quite a kick out of this for years; they always laugh when I throw punches in the air. I get so into the sport that when matches are over I need a massage! I am absolutely worn out.

Several years ago, I was given ringside tickets to the rematch between Sugar Ray Leonard and Roberto Duran at the Superdome in New Orleans. I took my family with me and made a little vacation out of this trip. They stayed at the hotel while I took my seat at the match. I was thrilled and could hardly wait for the fight of a lifetime. As my adrenaline started pumping, a man who looked like a high roller from Las Vegas took a seat next to me. I nicknamed him Amarillo Slim. On the other side of me was a guy who was decked out to the nines and looked as cool as they come. I called him Super Fly.

In a matter of seconds, we started talking about who we were rooting for. They both asked me whose side I was on and I told them Sugar Ray. Super Fly agreed with my choice and Amarillo Slim told us he was rooting for our opponent. As the lights started blazing and the announcers came out to introduce the two fighters, Amarillo Slim leaned over and slyly asked me, "How much do you want to bet, buddy?" I told him that I was a preacher who likes boxing but didn't bet. He was okay with that and then cocked his body toward Super Fly and asked him, "Hey, you. I betcha $5,000 that Duran beats Sugar Ray!" Super Fly thought for a minute and upped the ante, "Only $5,000? You must not be that confident. Make it $10,000 and I'm in!"

In the middle of all this, the two guys started wondering who was going to be the holder of the money. Amarillo Slim came up with the perfect solution and said, "Let the preacher hold the money. We can count on him!" Before I knew what was happening, my coat pockets were bulging with $10,000 cash in each pocket. I got a little worried thinking of the many cameras in the place. I hoped nobody would recognize me and make a hasty assumption that I was in the middle of a drug deal or something.

Right before the bell clanged and the first round started, the celebrated Mohammed Ali gracefully took a seat in the row in front of mine. This about clinched my excitement. I felt like a sugar-deprived kid in a candy store. The next thing you know, Sugar Ray was frustrating Duran almost immediately after the bell echoed in our ears. By the eighth round the real drama unfolded. Duran, one of the greatest lightweight champions in the world, just quit with the words *"No mas"* pouring out of his swollen lips. His manager began to plead with him to continue fighting, but Duran refused to listen. The crowd erupted in an uproar and the entire place went crazy. A bruised, battered and self-defeated Duran kept repeating, *"No mas. No mas.* I'm done. I quit." As fights broke out throughout the crowd, I quickly gave both Super Fly and Amarillo Slim their money back and made a mad dash toward safety.

What's my point? Roberto Duran, a professional boxer, quit. I'm not talking about a man who was a novice in the sport; I'm talking about a champion. A legendary champion. He did what he was trained *not* to do—he quit. Those of us who have been in the word of faith for a long time are likewise not supposed to quit. We have the authority in the name of Jesus. We do not have carnal weapons, but supernatural arsenals with the power to demolish strongholds. We have all come too far in the battle of faith to even think about quitting.

Called to Win

The society we live in today is shadowed by a quitter's mentality. The world quits at the drop of a hat. They quit when it gets too tough. They quit if they don't like their job. They quit if they don't like their spouse. They quit if they are tired of trying to raise a family. Unfortunately, that same spirit has crept right over into the Church. There are too many Christians who waste their time whining and organizing pity parties when they need to jump up, brush the dust off their clothes and tell the devil, "If it's a fight you want, it's a fight you're going to get. And when the dust settles, believe you me, God and I will triumph!"

When I was a little boy, my daddy told me never to run from a fight. I got picked on a lot when I was younger because I was real small in stature. There were plenty of bullies raring to pick a fight with me because beating me would be easy. My dad, who boxed in the Navy during World War II, taught me how to box and defend myself. I had no choice but to learn how to fight; my father would not let me quit. When I got older and became a believer, I became acquainted with a new opponent, the devil. I learned that his mission was to steal, kill and destroy. I am grateful for my father's lesson in never giving up because I took the same no-quit attitude and used it to defend myself against an enemy who prowls around like a roaring lion.

The society we live in today is shadowed by a quitter's mentality. That same spirit has crept right over into the Church.

Let's look at what God said in the book of Isaiah: "Behold, I have created the smith that bloweth the coals in the fire, and that bringeth forth an instrument for his work; and I have created the waster to destroy" (Isa. 54:16, *KJV*). In this passage the "waster" is a reference to Lucifer, the devil. Recognize that God says He created him. When God created Lucifer, he was not known as the waster or the destroyer; he was known as an anointed cherub. He was a heavenly being. But the Bible also says that iniquity was found in him. Lucifer wanted to exalt himself above the Most High God and led a third of the angelic hosts against His kingdom. God retaliated by casting him out, and Lucifer then became known as Satan. What's most important to remember is that God didn't create the devil to waste and destroy. He fell from grace on his own merit.

Verse 17 continues, "No weapon that is formed against thee shall prosper." God is simply saying, "I created Satan; and since I created him; I take full responsibility for his actions. I promise you if he forms a weapon against you, it shall not prosper. It shall not succeed." Those of you who are parents have experienced (many times, I'm sure) the frustration of watching your kids misbehave. Say one of your children starts throwing rocks at a neighbor's window and breaks the glass. The neighbor will be justifiably upset and likely to come running to you, the parent, to fix the problem. Now, did you create your child to throw rocks at people's homes? Of course not. But are you responsible for the damage? Absolutely! In the same way, God is responsible for Satan's actions, and He promises us that the devil's efforts to destroy us will not succeed. God has assured us that failure and defeat are not in our future. What is in our future? Triumph, winning, overcoming, ruling and reigning.

Jesus said it this way: "These things have I spoken unto you, that in me ye might have peace. In the world ye shall have tribulation: but be of good cheer; I have overcome the world" (John 16:33, KJV). Notice He said, "In the world ye shall have tribulation . . ." Challenges are inevitable. Weapons will be formed against us. Trials will come. Tribulations will be part of our life experience. But the bigger picture is that these things do not have the power to destroy us. The conjunction "but" is our saving grace: "*but* be of good cheer"; we can overcome all of those things. The *Amplified Bible* states this passage with a greater emphasis: "In the world you have tribulation and trials and distress and frustration; but be of good cheer [take courage; be confident, certain, undaunted]! For I have overcome the world. [I have deprived it of power to harm you and have conquered it for you]." What is Jesus saying? You have been called to battle and you have been destined to win.

The Bible tells us, "though a righteous man falls seven times, he rises again" (Prov. 24:16, *NIV*). My philosophy has always been:

If the devil knocks you down seven times, then get up eight. Quit giving your mind room to accept defeat. Quit talking about failure. Quit talking about defeat. Quit talking about how you can't take it anymore. Get up and declare to your adversary, "It's not over until I say it's over, and it's not over until I win!"

This message fires me up. I can almost hear the theme song from the *Rocky* film ringing in my ears. It makes me feel like Rocky Balboa and reminds me of a scene in *Rocky II*. Rocky's health is failing him after his first bout with Apollo Creed, and he retires from fighting at the same time his wife, Adrian, becomes pregnant. Apollo is not about to back down from his demands for a rematch and puts an overwhelming amount of pressure on Rocky. Rocky ends up accepting the challenge, but Adrian refuses to support his decision.

Some time before the fight, Adrian gives birth to their son and slips into a coma after experiencing severe complications from the delivery. Rocky is beside himself. He refuses to leave her side and spends time in the hospital chapel when forced out of her room by the nurses. Adrian remains unconscious for several days; and Rocky is hunched over her bedside, reading her stories and even poems that he's written for her. He tells his comatose wife, "I'm going to be here when you wake up."

When Adrian wakes up and regains her strength, and as they are cradling their newborn baby in their arms, Rocky tells her he is willing to give up his dream of fighting Apollo. He will do whatever she wants him to do. Adrian pauses for a minute and whispers, "There is one thing I want you to do for me . . . win!" And as loud bells kick off the inspirational theme song in the background, a wide-eyed Adrian repeats her request to her champion husband, "Win!"

When I watched this movie in the theater with my wife and a few friends of ours, I got so pumped up I accidentally hit a guy who was sitting in front of me! Think about your life for a minute. That popular song needs to be blaring in the background of your life right now. You may need to stand up and tell the devil, "This is the last time you are going to torment me. This is the last sleepless night I will ever have in my life. This is the last time you are going to damage my marriage. This is the last time you are going to control my children. This is the last time you are going to steal my finances. This is the last time you are going to rob me of good health. In the name of Jesus, I declare a state of war! I declare that I am destined to win!"

We need to start declaring war on our enemy. We need to put on the armor of God and never take it off. We have to march into battle knowing that our victory has already been settled. It has been guaranteed. It has been written, "You will win! You will triumph!" The book of Psalms encourages us to "Shout unto God with the voice of triumph. . . . He [God] shall subdue the people under us, and the nations under our feet" (Ps. 47:1,3, *KJV*). The voice of triumph didn't come after the subduing; it came first. You may be facing real and difficult challenges, or a fight of faith of some sort; but believe in your heart that you are destined to win.

Declare those truths and lift up a voice of triumph. You shall not be defeated!

3

WAKE UP THE MIGHTY MEN AND WOMEN

Waking Up

"Proclaim ye this among the Gentiles; Prepare war, wake up the mighty men, let all the men of war draw near; let them come up" (Joel 3:9, *KJV*). In this Scripture, Joel is telling the mighty men and women of God, the great warriors who had gone to sleep, to wake up and fight.

That verse astounded me when I first read it. I was greatly impressed that we cannot play church anymore. This is the day of a great people, and they are called the Body of Christ. This is the hour for the Church. This is the hour for the mighty warriors of God to wake up.

Years ago, I was supposed to preach in my hometown of Fort Worth. I had been involved in some board meetings that day, and when I got home, I was exhausted. I was going to lie down and take a nap before I preached that night. I fell into one of those deep sleeps. The minute I hit the pillow, I was gone. An hour later, I felt somebody shaking me. It was my oldest daughter. I could barely make it out of my sleep, and I heard her say, "Daddy, it's time to get up." I only slept for a short time, but it felt like I could have slept for a month. When I was first awakened, I wasn't of use to anybody. When I put my feet on the floor, I had no idea where I was. I didn't know what time of day it was. I didn't even know what day it was. But still, I was awake.

This is exactly where the Church is spiritually—a sleeping giant that has finally awakened. We might not know where we are, but we're about to get there. I want you to know that the scales are going to come off of our eyes and we're going to see exactly what

God is doing. We're going to find out what the strategies are. We're going to be sensitive to the Spirit. We're going to be so alive that the devil is going to wish he had never attacked us.

**This is the day of a great people
called the Body of Christ. This is the hour for
the mighty warriors of God to wake up.**

Now what we've got to do is get the sleep out of our eyes. We've got to clear our minds. We've got to keep hearing the instructions of the Holy Spirit. We've got to keep flowing with God. And as we keep doing these things, we're going to see what God sees. We're going to have the mind of God. We're going to think like He thinks, talk like He talks, fight like He fights and win like He wins!

The Problem with God's Army

The prophet Joel wrote something very powerful: "Blow ye the trumpet in Zion, and sound an alarm in my holy mountain: let all the inhabitants of the land tremble: for the day of the LORD cometh, for it is nigh at hand" (Joel 2:1, *KJV*). He starts off with the command to blow the trumpet. Have you noticed that the phrase "blow the trumpet" is mentioned several times in the Bible, particularly in the Old Testament? There are many different types of trumpets mentioned and they all mean something different. The jubilee trumpet, for example, means freedom and redemption. The ram's horn signifies a covenant.

The trumpet mentioned in Joel, however, is a battle cry. Joel is saying, "Get ready for all-out warfare like you've never been in before." It's much like the bugle blower you see in those Old West Army movies. When the Indians pull a surprise attack, you hear the bugle blower sounding that particular series of notes, and all of a sudden, you see a bunch of men coming out of their tents, pulling up their suspenders, grabbing their rifles and getting ready for a battle. God is blowing the trumpet today. He is calling us to prepare for war. Christianity is not about fun and games. It's a fight to the finish. But let's get real—most of us aren't ready for battle. What is wrong with God's army today?

We Don't Know Who Our Enemy Is

We have been so ignorant that sometimes we don't even know who our enemy is. That's a very sad thing. The Church is fighting one another. Do the following words sound familiar?

"Do you believe in speaking in tongues?"
"No."
"Well, you're going to hell."

"Are you a Baptist?"
"No."
"Then we don't want you in our camp."

"Do you believe once saved always saved?"
"No."
"You must be of the devil."

Words like that thrill our enemy. The devil just sits back and lets us kill off each other and then takes the spoil for himself. Jesus said, "Any kingdom divided against itself will be ruined, and a house divided against itself will fall" (Luke 11:17, *NIV*). The devil took that verse and is using it to destroy the Body of Christ. He is saying, "I'm going to divide their house. I'm going to get one side believing one thing and the other side believing something else. I'm going to get them fighting with one another, and eventually their kingdom will fall."

We Don't Know What Our Weapons Are

God wants a very highly organized and sophisticated army that He can depend on. He needs soldiers who are highly trained and skilled. He needs us to understand tactics, warfare and the weapons of battle. So many Christians don't even know what their weapons are. Speaking in tongues is a powerful weapon, but many people think it's only a sign of being Pentecostal. No! It's a powerful weapon to pull down strongholds. Also, the name of Jesus is another powerful weapon. The Bible tells us, "at the name of Jesus every knee should bow, of things in heaven, and things in earth, and things under the earth; and that every tongue should confess that Jesus Christ is Lord, to the glory of God the Father" (Phil. 2:10-11, *KJV*). All principalities, powers, might and dominion are under that name. The name of Jesus is far above and highly exalted above everything. Another powerful weapon is the Bible—God's Word. It is a sword. You don't play with swords; you fight with them. God doesn't want us thinking that the Bible is just a book. It's one of our weapons against the Enemy.

We Don't Listen

The armies in the natural realm court-martial people who don't obey commands. By all rights, God should have courtmartialed us years ago. He gives us orders that we don't think much about. We'll do it when we want to. When it feels comfortable. When we get around to it. Try saying that to the leaders of the United States Army. If a company commander tells you you're going on a 20-mile hike at 4:00 in the morning, you wouldn't tell him, "Listen, I didn't get much sleep last night, so I don't think I'm going to go. Send someone else." Believe me; that will not go over well. We Christians know what we need to do, but we don't want to listen. Why do we think we can do whatever we want whenever we feel like it in the most important army of all—God's army?

We have been in such a slumber that the devil has been able to take control of everything. The time has come to wake up and fight back.

We've Fallen Asleep

We have been in such a slumber in days past that the devil has been able to take control of everything. We sit in our living rooms, for instance, and spend hours in front of the TV watching junk. You can hardly turn on any program without seeing some kind of adultery, fornication or perversion.

It's time to wake up, folks! It's time for us to shake ourselves and realize that the devil has set us back somewhat. He's taken territory; he's taken ground that should have been God's all along. The time has come to wake up and fight back. It's time to take back everything that was stolen from us and claim it back as God's property.

Where Do We Start?

We're not going to wake up and win by being religious. This is war. We have to make sacrifices. We have to get right in the middle of it. We have to get right in the heat of it. So, where do we start?

Blowing the Trumpet

We need to blow the trumpet and attack. The only thing that is going to get the devil's attention is blowing the trumpet and declaring war against him.

I can remember the day I told the devil, "In the name of Jesus, you're not lord of this house. You're not lord of my life. You're not lord of my kids. In Jesus' name, you get out and don't you ever come back, because I'm fed up with your lies." He knew I meant business. As long as you keep doing nothing except gripe, complain and whine about what you think God let happen to you, the devil is going to beat your brains out. The moment you get fed up with being oppressed, the moment you put your foot down, the moment you take on your spiritual weapons is the moment he'll have to flee.

There were times I had to literally grab myself by the ear, pull myself up out of the chair, sofa or bed, look into a mirror, point my finger and say, "Jerry Savelle, you listen to me. You straighten up. You quit listening to the lies of the devil. You do what you know the Bible says, and I don't want to hear another negative word out of you. Do you understand?" Do you know what I was doing? I was blowing my trumpet. I was sounding the alarm in my own life. Every one of us has to blow our trumpet and let the devil know that we mean business.

Training

What good is a soldier if he's not trained? The Army doesn't take some civilian, stick an M14 rifle in his hand and say, "Go get the enemy." He has to go through training. He needs boot camp. It's not fun; it's not comfortable; but it's necessary. Well, God has His own boot camp. He intended from day one for us to get into training because, whether we've recognized it or not, God considers us soldiers, and we're going to war.

In military boot camp, if at the end of eight weeks of training you don't pass the exams, you get recycled and have to go through it all over again. In God's army, if you do what God tells you to do, training doesn't take all that long. But most of us complain and whine. "I don't want to keep studying the Word." "I don't want to keep praying." "I don't want to go to church." "I'm sick." "I'm tired." "I'm sick and tired."

Boot camp is vital. God is aiming to make an army out of us, and He can't afford to have a bunch of quitters as soldiers. We have to hang in there. Why? Because God said so, and He knows best. You're going to have it do it sooner or later, so you might as well make up your mind now to learn what God is trying to teach you in boot camp so that you can graduate and get on to AIT.

Advanced Individual Training

This is where the Body of Christ belongs right now. We ought to have graduated out of boot camp, had a glorious ceremony and moved right on into AIT. Here is where the Holy Spirit begins to make specialists out of us. Here is where He tells you what your job is because you can now be trusted. You've got a soldier's intellect. You take pride in your uniform. You're ready for war.

I remember the day I graduated from basic training. Oh, what a relief it was to have all that behind me! The minute I was done with basic, I was sent off to AIT. All of a sudden, I wanted to be a soldier, and I wanted to be the best one I could possibly be. The Army was now going to train me to become what they wanted me to become. In my case, they put me in a 4.2 mortar platoon and wanted to make a gunner out of me. In an instant, I got interested in how to become a gunner. I got interested in how to do it right. I started listening to what the leaders said to me. I started watching more closely during the instruction time. I never will forget how proud I was when I aced the final exam.

**God is aiming to make an army out of us,
and He can't have quitters as soldiers.**

You and I are in AIT. God is making specialists out of us. He knows how to train people to do what He wants them to do. If you're a pastor, quit trying to be a teacher. If you're a teacher, quit trying to be an evangelist. If you're an evangelist, quit trying to be a prophet. Be what God has trained you to be.

When I was stationed at Fort Dix, New Jersey, there were many times when some of the guys coming out of Vietnam would come through before they got discharged. Whenever the Airborne Rangers and Green Berets passed through, everyone stopped and stared. There was something different about them—they meant business. These were guys who went through extensive training to become the best they could possibly be and excel under tremendous adversity. I believe God's got some spiritual Airborne Rangers. I believe God's got some spiritual Green Berets. I believe God's got some people that He causes to go through more extensive training than others.

Some of you go through things that other people don't go through and you don't understand why. God's trying to make a mighty man or woman out of you. He'll even use the trials that Satan puts you through. The reason is, He wants to make a winner out of you!

Let's look at a powerful story in the Bible. "Now these are they that came to David to Ziklag, while he yet kept himself close because of Saul the son of Kish: and they were among the mighty men, helpers of the war. They were armed with bows, and *could use both the right hand and the left* in hurling stones and shooting arrows out of a bow, even of Saul's brethren of Benjamin" (1 Chron. 12:1-2, *KJV*, emphasis added). This passage has several references to the description of the mighty men of David. I want to talk about a few.

I asked the Lord one day, "What does it mean for us today to be able to use both our left and our right hands?" God shared with me that it meant being able to adapt to any situation. Why is that important to us today? There may be times when you'll be called on by the Holy Spirit to do things that you've never done before and, when you are, you had better be able to use both hands; or in other words, be adaptable. Mighty men and women who can use both hands are never caught off guard. They are alert at all times.

"And of the Gadites there separated themselves unto David into the hold to the wilderness men of might, and men of war fit for the battle, that could handle shield and buckler, *whose faces were like the faces of lions*, and *were as swift as the roes upon the mountains*" (1 Chron. 12:8, *KJV*, emphasis added). These warriors had faces of lions. To me that means they were determined. If you ever watch a person with a determined expression on his face, you will notice that expression never changes. Every vein in his entire body expresses determination. God needs people like that. He needs soldiers who are determined to win. He also needs people who are unafraid. These mighty men of David had the heart of a champion on the inside of them, and they were determined to win no matter the cost.

This verse also says the men "were as swift as the roes upon the mountains." I see a mighty man or woman who is swift as a roe as having diligence. They are never lazy. They never quit. While they may experience some setbacks, they are quick to recover. They might get hedged in, but they never get crushed.

"And of the children of Issachar, which were *men that had understanding of the times*, to know what Israel ought to do; the heads of them were two hundred; and all their brethren were at their commandment" (1 Chron. 12:32, *KJV*, emphasis added). This description tells me these mighty men were full of wisdom. It also means to me that they never got cut off from headquarters. God needs us to know what to do. The only way we're going to know what to do in war is to be linked up with headquarters.

"Of Zebulun, such as went forth to battle, *expert in war*, with all instruments of war, fifty thousand, which could keep rank: *they were not of double heart*" (1 Chron. 12:33, *KJV*, emphasis added). These guys were skillful. They were experts in war. God wants us to be experts. We need to practice what we preach; we need to walk the walk and talk the talk. The Bible also says these men "were not of double heart." What does that mean? It means they were unwavering and were willing to fight for a long time.

"All these men of war, that could keep rank, came with a perfect heart to Hebron, to make David king over all Israel: and all the rest also of Israel were *of one heart* to make David king" (1 Chron. 12:38, *KJV*, emphasis added). These men "were of one heart." They were knit together. There was no strife among them. Together they became an unbeatable force. As the Body of Christ, we need to come together and quit fighting over stupid things. We need to be of one heart.

When It's Just Too Much

"In the last days perilous times shall come" (2 Tim. 3:1, *KJV*). The *Amplified Bible* calls this "times of great stress and trouble." We are living in stressful times. That's the reason so many people have lost their joy and are not experiencing something fresh in their life today. They are so beat down they can't even work up enough initiative to go seek God. Sometimes you just get tired. Life can be too much. But don't give up. God is on your side.

Paul reminds us, "I have strength for all things in Christ who empowers me [I am ready for anything and equal to anything through Him who infuses inner strength into me; I am self-sufficient in Christ's sufficiency]" (Phil. 4:13, *AMP*). Without Christ there is no empowerment. We don't have the power to do what we need to do on our own. We need to come to the place where we say, "God, I cannot do this anymore. I can't do all these things You've given to me to do. I can't carry the load of this anymore. It's too big, it's too much." We need Christ to work in us to become the mighty men and women He wants us to be.

We need Christ to work in us to become the mighty men and women that He wants us to be.

God wants His people to experience a fresh infusion of the Holy Spirit. Paul gave us the idea in Ephesians that we are to be filled with the Holy Spirit (see Eph. 5:18). The literal Greek translation of this text means "to be filled and keep on being filled." This is not a one-time deal. It is continual. You've got to get into a position where the Holy Spirit is infusing into you His strength and the mind, the ways and ideas of God. All it takes is one *God idea* to change your life, change your finances and change everything around you. But you have to get into a position to receive it. So how do we get this fresh infusion? I'd like to share with you seven decisions you need to make to experience this refreshing and keep being filled with the Holy Spirit.

1. Be in God's Presence

This is a simple one. If you're not in His presence, you won't receive that refreshing.

2. Crave God

God gives this infusion only to those who crave it. It's not going to happen to you because it's happening to me. The Bible tells us, "Seek, inquire of and for the Lord, and crave Him and His strength (His might and inflexibility to temptation); seek and require His face and His presence [continually] evermore" (Ps. 105:4, *AMP*).

When we get up in the morning, we need to crave God. We need to put God first in our lives. The minute our eyes open, we need to seek Him. We need to praise Him. We need to worship Him. It will make your coffee taste better. It will cause you to sing in the shower. Getting close to God is as easy as getting close to somebody you admire and respect. In fact, it's easier to get closer to God than some people you'd like to be close to. You can be close to God anytime you want. He's not too busy for you. There is no line at the throne room. You don't have to wait for a million people to get out of the way before He has time for you.

When you begin to look at God as your indispensable necessity, there is an intense longing for Him. King David gave us an example of that craving:

My life dissolves and weeps itself away for heaviness; raise me up and strengthen me according to [the promises of] Your word. Remove from me the way of falsehood and unfaithfulness [to You], and graciously impart Your law to me. I have chosen the way of truth and faithfulness; Your ordinances have I set before me. I cleave to Your testimonies; O Lord, put me not to shame! I will [not merely walk, but] run the way of Your commandments, when You give me a heart that is willing. Teach me, O Lord, the way of Your statutes, and I will keep it to the end [steadfastly]. Give me understanding, that I may keep Your law; yes, I will observe it with my whole heart. Make me go in the path of Your commandments, for in them do I delight. Incline my heart to Your testimonies and not to covetousness (robbery, sensuality, unworthy riches). Turn away my eyes from beholding vanity (idols and idolatry); and restore me to vigorous life and health in Your ways (Ps. 119:28-37, *AMP*).

Notice that David wrote, "Turn away my eyes from beholding vanity (idols and idolatry); and restore me to vigorous life and health in Your ways." What he was saying was, "Turn my eyes away from distractions and give me a fresh infusion of the Holy Spirit." A few verses later, David came to a realization that he couldn't do this on his own. "I have seen that everything [human] has its limits and end [no matter how extensive, noble, and excellent]; but Your commandment is exceedingly broad and extends without limits [into eternity]" (Ps. 119:96, *AMP*).

When you crave God fully, you will get to a place where you realize that everything human has its limits. You can't do it on your own. You can't think up all by yourself how to overcome all of the adversity and trials you are experiencing. You can't figure out how to do all of this because everything human has its limits. No matter how extensive, how noble, how excellent, or how intelligent we are, we are limited. This is why God says, "Not by might, nor by power, but by my spirit" (Zech. 4:6, *KJV*). If you don't come to this realization, you are going to be in serious trouble, because neither the world nor the devil is going to let up any time soon. The warfare will intensify. Know that God is greater.

3. Deepen Your Relationship with God

Renew your quest to know God intimately by making a commitment to deepen your relationship with the Holy Spirit. There is a new awareness of needing to become closer to God. I believe that the closer we get to the Second Coming, then the closer to God you and I must get. "Draw nigh to God, and he will draw nigh unto you" (Jas. 4:8, *KJV*). I like how the *Amplified Version* states it: "Get close to God and He will come close to you." If you take a step toward God, He'll take a step toward you.

4. Press in to Jesus

What do I mean by "press in"? Let me give you an example. Do you remember the biblical story about the woman with the issue of blood? For years she suffered with the disease. When she discovered Jesus was going to be in town, she did whatever she needed to do to get near Him. She fought crowds of people to just touch Him. She was convinced one touch of His garment would heal her.

She had her mind made up. She didn't care how many people were standing around Jesus. She didn't care if she might get trampled. She didn't care what the consequences might be. She didn't even care that the ruler of the synagogue was standing right next to Jesus. This man had the authority to stone her because, under Levitical law, she was considered to be an unclean woman. She had no business being in that crowd, but she didn't care. She pressed in. She knew that the presence of God was available. How desperate are you to touch Jesus today?

When you crave God fully, you will get to a place where you realize that everything human has its limits.

This story also reminds me of the story of a tax collector named Zacchaeus. He, too, was desperate to see Jesus. He heard Jesus was coming his way, and he made up his mind that he was going to see Him. If you are familiar with the story, you know that Zacchaeus was a short man. He would never be able to see Jesus in a crowd, because he was so small. What did this man do? He climbed up a sycamore tree and shouted at Jesus to capture His attention. Jesus heard him and that night they had dinner together. Zacchaeus is the man Jesus went home with because Zacchaeus pressed in. Jesus wants to sit at your table too, but you've got to press in. How hungry are you for God? Are you going to let people stand in your way? Are you going to follow the crowd? Or are you going to get into a position to receive?

5. Rekindle Your Desire for the Word

If the Bible is no longer exciting for you, then you need to rekindle your desire for it. Every time I get up in the morning, I am so excited to study the Word of God. I'm hungry for new revelation. I've been a student of the Word for 40 years, but I am hungrier for revelation knowledge now than I've ever been before. This is not just so that I will have more sermons to preach, but also so that I can know Him more fully and deeply. If you don't feel that way right now, don't feel bad. Just ask the Lord to give you a fresh desire to read His Word and understand it in a whole new way.

6. Keep Your Life Pure

"The Lord shall utter his voice before his army: for his camp is very great: for he is strong that executeth his word: for the day of the Lord is great and very terrible; and who can abide it? Therefore also now, saith the Lord, turn ye even to me with all your heart, and with fasting, and with weeping, and with mourning: And rend your heart, and not your garments, and turn unto the Lord your God: for he is gracious and merciful, slow to anger, and of great kindness, and repenteth him of the evil. Who knoweth if he will return and repent, and leave a blessing behind him; even a meat offering and a drink offering unto the Lord your God?" (Joel 2:11-14, *KJV*).

What does keeping pure mean? Simply that we've got to clean up our lives. God is saying, "I don't want an outward appearance of holiness; I want an inward holiness. I don't want an outward appearance of servitude; I want it coming from your heart. I don't want it just looking as though you're serving Me; I want you truly and fully serving Me." It means stop playing church. Stop the religious games. Don't be satisfied with the norm anymore. Clean your life up. Demand of yourself that sin has got to go; strife has got to go; bitterness has got to go; jealousy has got to go. We don't have time to play around with those things anymore. They are luxuries of the flesh, and God wants us to take authority over them. He wants us to take authority over our minds and become holy and mighty men and women who are fit to serve in His army.

7. Give Yourself to Prayer and Intercession

A mighty man or woman is a person who is strong in prayer. His or her attitude is to pray first before doing anything else. A lot of people use prayer as a last resort. When any problem comes up, they try this and that, and it is only after this and that doesn't work that they decide to pray. Mighty men and women know to pray first. They are strong in prayer and strong in faith.

It's time to wake up! You need to realize that we're already on the winning team and what God needs is for all of us to prepare for war. If you listen closely, you're going to hear, in the Spirit, His trumpet. You're going to hear the battle cry. Prepare yourself. Turn to God with all your heart.

Get ready for battle! Prepare for your greatest warfare. Prepare also for your greatest victories. You're called to battle, but destined to win.

4

OUTWITTING YOUR ADVERSARY

What's the Devil's Plan?

I've had the privilege of traveling all over the world. Because we have a staff in Africa, I've been all over that continent preaching, training leaders and building churches. When I went to South Africa one time, I took what's called a "camera safari" to a very famous place called Mala Mala. One of the tour guides on this trip told me that the encounter most sought is to watch a lion stalk his prey and actually witness the kill. While that may not sound too glamorous, it is quite an adventurous experience. It's fascinating to watch what the lion goes through—how subtle, persistent and patient he is—when he stalks his prey.

Another interesting event is watching a giraffe attempt to get a drink of water. The reason is not only because the giraffe is so tall and has to get in position to drink through several awkward movements, but also because this is a time when it is most vulnerable for the lion to attack it. On this safari, the ranger assigned to me drove me to an area where we sat in a bush waiting for this one giraffe to get a drink of water. We waited for more than two hours!

When I saw what the giraffe had to go through, I was amazed. This animal's legs are so long that it can't just bend down and get a drink. It has to spread its legs a little bit at a time while looking around and listening for any unusual noises, like the stalking of a lion. If it thinks the coast is clear, it'll spread its legs a little bit more and then look up and around again. When it finally gets its legs spread out as far as they can go and bends its knees where it can get a drink, the giraffe is now at a very vulnerable position. That's the best time for lions to attack. Keep in mind, the lion is a very patient animal. It'll wait and wait, and then wait some more until the giraffe is in a perfect position of vulnerability. Then it'll attack. This is exactly what the devil does.

"Be sober, be vigilant; because your adversary the devil, as a roaring lion, walketh about, seeking whom he may devour" (1 Pet. 5:8, *KJV*). Peter says that we must be on guard because the devil goes around like a roaring lion. Notice he doesn't say that he *is* a roaring lion. That's very important to understand. Just because the devil can prowl around and roar or stalk his prey like a lion doesn't make him one.

Paul wrote, "Lest Satan should get an advantage of us: for we are not ignorant of his devices" (2 Cor. 2:11, *KJV*). Paul is telling us to be mindful of the devil's tricks. Now I'm not suggesting that we spend all of our time studying the devil, but at the same time, if you are naive as to how he operates, you're going to be at a disadvantage. In competitive sports, not only do two teams play each other, but they also spend much time practicing on the field going through basic fundamentals. They will spend much time exercising and practicing their game plan on and off the field. They learn as much as they can about their opponent. They do all of these things to gain an advantage against their opponent. And the team that knows the most about how the other team operates and reacts will more than likely be the team that wins.

In this verse, the word "advantage" in the Greek means a favorable position. It also means superiority. The devil is always looking for an advantage. He's always looking for a favorable position. He's always looking for superiority. The only way for us to be defeated by the devil is if he gains a favorable position. So how does he do this? He studies your weaknesses. He finds out what it is that causes you to break under pressure. He's not going to attack you in your strong areas. If alcohol, cigarettes or lust are not temptations for you, he's not going to use those things to tempt you. He's much too crafty for that.

The team that knows the most about how the other team operates and reacts will more than likely be the team that wins.

Satan is a master deceiver. One of his mightiest weapons is deception. "Now the serpent was more subtle than any beast of the field which the Lord God had made" (Gen. 3:1, *KJ21*). The word "subtle" means crafty or seductive. In the Hebrew translation, the word "serpent" means to hiss, to whisper or to enchant. That's the way the devil attempts to gain a favorable position. Did you ever notice that one of his favorite tactics is to whisper things to discourage you? How many of you wake up in the morning, barely have one eyelid open and he's already hissing in your ear. "It's not gonna work." "You're gonna lose your job." "You're never going to get healed." "You'll never receive your miracle."

Here's an example of how Satan did this to Jesus. Luke writes that Jesus had been fasting for 40 days in the wilderness and that during the whole time He was tempted by the devil. What was the devil looking for? A favorable position so that he could defeat Jesus. After the 40 days ended, the Bible tells us "[Jesus] afterward hungered" (Luke 4:2, *KJV*). If Jesus was hungry, any opportunity to eat could have constituted a real temptation, so the devil used that to his advantage.

"And the devil said unto Him, If Thou be the Son of God, command this stone that it be made bread" (Luke 4:3, *KJV*). Notice how Jesus answered back. "It is written, That man shall not live by bread alone, but by every word of God" (Luke 4:4, *KJV*). How did Jesus resist the temptation? By using the Word of God. Jesus did not say, "Get thee behind me, Satan, for I am the Son of God." No, He based His success on something Moses wrote many years before. If Jesus can win quoting Old Testament Scripture, then we can win quoting the New Testament. It worked for Jesus, and it can work for us.

Let's look at the next few verses.

> And the devil, taking him up into an high mountain, shewed unto him all the kingdoms of the world in a moment of time. And the devil said unto him, All this power will I give thee, and the glory of them: for that is delivered unto me; and to whomsoever I will I give it. If thou therefore wilt worship me, all shall be thine. And Jesus answered and said unto him, Get thee behind me, Satan: for it is written, Thou shalt worship the Lord thy God, and him only shalt thou serve (Luke 4:5-8, *KJV*).

If the devil didn't get Jesus the first time, he was certain to try again. The devil was running all over the place trying to gain a favorable position. Just because you ran the devil off this morning, don't think he won't be back. The Bible does tell us that if we resist him, he'll flee. But he doesn't flee permanently. He'll be back. If the devil couldn't get you to fight with your spouse this morning, he'll try to get you to fight with her tonight. If that doesn't work, he'll attack your finances. If he can't get you there, he'll try to stop your car from running.

The devil came after Jesus a third time. "And he [the devil] brought him [Jesus] to Jerusalem, and set him on a pinnacle of the temple, and said unto him, If thou be the Son of God, cast thyself down from hence: For it is written, He shall give his angels charge over thee, to keep thee: And in their hands they shall bear thee up, lest at any time thou dash thy foot against a stone. And Jesus answering said unto him, It is said, Thou shalt not tempt the Lord thy God" (Luke 4:9-12, *KJV*). Once again, Jesus kept the Word of God in front of Him in order to keep the adversary from having an advantage over Him. We need to do the same thing. We need to continually confess the Word of God every time the devil tries to have his way with us.

Finally the devil gave up, but not for long. "And when the devil had ended all the temptation, he departed from him for a season" (Luke 4:13, *KJV*). One translation says the devil left Jesus "for a more opportune time." If he doesn't find a favorable position or an advantage in your life, he'll leave for just enough time to get you to start relaxing, and thinking, *Well, hallelujah! I won that one.* But don't let your guard down. Be sober. Be vigilant. At all times.

The Power of Knowledge Against the Devil's Deceptions

The book of Genesis tells us the story of two brothers, Jacob and Esau. Jacob was trying to take their father's blessing away from his brother, Esau, who was entitled to it as the firstborn. Esau was just about to receive it because their father, Isaac, was on his deathbed. Esau went to Isaac, who was practically blind, and asked him, "What can I do for you?" His father said, "Go and get me my favorite venison meat, prepare it the way that I like, and bring it to me. Then I will eat it, give you my blessing, and then I will die" (see Gen. 27:3-4). In obedience to his father, Esau left to do that.

Their mother, Rebecca, who considered Jacob her favorite, had already been scheming about how they could rob Esau of his blessing. She came up with an idea for Jacob to pretend he was Esau because Isaac, blind as a bat, wouldn't be able to tell the difference. She covered Jacob, who had smooth skin, with the smell and hair of animals so that he would feel as hairy as his brother and carry the same kind of smell. You might say that Rebecca and Jacob were able to gain a favorable position.

So unknowingly, Isaac conferred the blessing on Jacob, the blessing that rightfully belonged to Esau. Esau came back with the meal and told his father, "Here is your food, now bless me." Isaac was confused and asked him who he was. "I'm your son Esau," the tricked brother said. And all of a sudden Esau began to realize that his brother Jacob had deceived him. Esau was obviously very torn up about this and he begged his father, "Isn't there anything you can do? Can't you reverse it? Can't you take it back?" But Isaac couldn't do anything at all.

Genesis 27:35 tells us, "Thy brother came with subtlety, and hath taken away thy blessing" (*KJV*). This is descriptive of how our adversary, the devil, operates. He is very subtle. He is very crafty. He is a master deceiver. One of the major ways he deceives the Body of Christ is by keeping them ignorant of what is rightfully theirs. God said, "My people are destroyed for lack of knowledge" (Hos. 4:6, *KJV*).

**One of the major ways Satan deceives
the Body of Christ is by keeping them ignorant
of what is rightfully theirs.**

I don't know how you were affected by reading that verse, but when I read it back in 1969, when I made Jesus the Lord of my life, I began to really dig into the Bible and started to receive revelation from the Holy Spirit. Eventually, I became angry because I realized Christians had been lying to me all my life. Preachers had been lying to me all my life. I was told that God was my problem, not the devil. For instance, they were telling me that God would make me sick to teach me something. This was Satan's way to steal my health. He wanted me to believe a lie, but I refused.

I'll never forget one time when Carolyn and I were first married. She went to church all the time, but I didn't go very much. One morning, she left for church and I stayed home and worked on my hot rod. I was working on my '57 Chevy when all of a sudden the car fell off the jack and should have pinned me under it. Somehow I was not crushed, even though I should have been. But if I had been an inch or two thicker, it would have crushed me.

When Carolyn came home from church, I told her what happened. When she went back to church that night, she told someone that story, and you know what they said? They said God did it because I was skipping church. They said He was trying to teach me something. Are you kidding me? Honestly, do you think that made me want to jump up next Sunday morning and go to church? I wasn't interested in serving a God who wanted to kill me.

When I did start going to church, I wouldn't just sit in the pew and go along with their religious traditions, and I didn't fit in their religious box. I challenged them with what the Word of God said. And let me tell you, they didn't like it one bit. They didn't like people who rocked the boat. But that's the way I am with the Word of God. I don't accept it just because somebody says that's the way it should be. I search it out for myself. My attitude is, "If God says it, then that settles it!"

God's people are destroyed for a lack of knowledge. One of the most seductive things the devil can do to a child of God is keep him or her ignorant. That's why God told Joshua to meditate on the Word by day and by night. If you do that, the mind of Christ is going to begin to function in your life. Knowledge is going to come. Revelation is going to come.

Jesus once asked His disciples, "Who do men say that I am?" " 'Well,' they replied, 'some say John the Baptist, some say Elijah, and others say Jeremiah or one of the other prophets.' Then he asked them, 'Who do you say I am?' Simon Peter answered, 'You are the Messiah, the Son of the living God.' Jesus replied, 'You are blessed, Simon son of John, because my Father in heaven has revealed this to you. You did not learn this from any human being' " (Matt. 16:13-17, *NLT*).

Jesus was talking to Peter about a knowledge that does not come through the five physical senses. He was talking about a knowledge that is revealed only by the Holy Spirit. Jesus finally said to Peter, "Upon this rock I will build my church, and all the powers of hell will not conquer it" (Matt. 16:18, *NLT*). When you are operating in revelation knowledge, the gates of hell cannot prevail against you!

It's obvious why Satan would want to keep us ignorant. He doesn't care if we're religious, just as long as we are spiritually oblivious. Religion is a worse dope than LSD, crack or cocaine. It's the worst dope a man can get because it dopes him into thinking he is doing something for God when he is doing nothing at all. We need to be studying the Bible and continually receiving revelation knowledge because we are dealing with an enemy who is trying to rob us of what rightfully belongs to us.

It is obvious why Satan would want to keep us ignorant. He doesn't care if we're religious, just as long as we are spiritually oblivious.

Had Isaac's eyes not been dimmed, Rebecca and Jacob would not have been able to pull off that stunt. If you are not spiritually dim, the devil can never pull off deception in your life. That's the reason the Bible says the entrance of God's Word gives light (see Ps. 119:130). The more of God's Word you have in you, the brighter the light is all around you. And the brighter the light is around you, the better and quicker you can spot the devil every time he shows up. He can't hide in the dark where you are concerned because you've got the light on.

Getting into the Word needs to be the most instinctive thing about you. When you get up in the morning, get into the Word. When you go to bed at night, get into the Word. In every situation, look to the Word. Getting into the Word is a good habit to develop. The more you continue in it, the more revelation you will receive. It's amazing how it works. For example, the more of God's Word you inject into your spirit regarding healing, the less you have to deal with sickness. The more of God's Word you inject into your spirit concerning prosperity, the better off you become financially.

Get Aggressive and Get Fed Up

The devil loves it when you are passive. It makes his job so much easier. But when you start getting aggressive, alarms go off in his domain. You become a prime target because you are now dangerous. You have become a threat to his operations. Isaac told Esau in Genesis 27:40, "And by thy sword shalt thou live . . . and it shall come to pass when thou shalt have the dominion, that thou shalt break his yoke from off thy neck." The *New International Version* puts it this way: "When you grow restless, you will throw his yoke from off your neck."

What does this mean? You are going to live with whatever you are going through until you get restless or fed up. Until you get fed up with being the tail, not the head; until you get fed up with being the sick, not the healed. Until you get fed up with being the broken, not the restored. Until you get fed up with being the broke, not the prosperous. It's only when you get fed up that you move toward action. If you're not spiritually restless, then you'll keep tolerating the devil lording it over you. The devil will keep pushing and pushing and pushing you until you totally give up; but if you ever get fed up, then he's in trouble.

Let's look at 2 Samuel and let me show you what I mean by "fed up." This passage of Scripture talks about the mighty men of David. I want you to notice their attitude. "These be the names of the mighty men whom David had: The Tachmonite that sat in the seat, chief among the captains; the same was Adino the Eznite: he lift up his spear against eight hundred, whom he slew at one time" (2 Sam. 23:8, *KJV*). This Adino guy got his fill of the Philistines. They pushed him too far. He got so fed up with them that he took his sword and he swung that thing around so that by the time it was all over, there were 800 Philistines stacked up around this man. Enough was enough for Adino.

Let's look at another one of David's men, one of my favorites. "And after him was Eleazar the son of Dodo the Ahohite, one of the three mighty men. . . . He arose and smote the Philistines until his hand was weary, and his hand clave unto the sword: and the LORD wrought a great victory that day; and the people returned after him only to spoil" (2 Sam. 23:9-10, *KJV*). Every time I read that verse I think there's hope for all of us. If it'll work for a Dodo, it'll work for all of us.

Eleazar, the son of Dodo, was pushed too far. He got fed up. When this guy got through with the Philistines, people literally had to pry his hand off the handle of his sword. You can push a Dodo too far. The next time the devil comes against you, tell him, "You have pushed this Dodo too far."

Here's the last guy. "And after him was Shammah the son of Agee the Hararite. And the Philistines were gathered together into a troop, where was a piece of ground full of lentils: and the people fled from the Philistines" (2 Sam. 23:11, *KJV*). I like to think of lentils as another name for beans. So we've got this young man named Shammah who owned a bean patch. The Philistines kept trampling down his beans to the point where he finally got fed up. What Shammah had wasn't all that much; it was just a little bean patch. But you know what? It was *his* bean patch. So he got fed up with the Philistines messing with his bean patch, and he stood right in the middle of it and killed the Philistines in defense of it. He declared war over his bean patch, and God gave him a great victory.

Think about your own life for a minute. You may be thinking that your house or your health or your finances or your spouse may not be much to anyone else but they do matter. If it's yours, defend it. Don't let the devil steal it. Energize your faith the next time the devil is trying to steal something of yours by calling it a bean patch, and act like Shammah. Tell the devil, "You are not taking my bean patch. You are not taking my blessing. You are not taking my inheritance. You are not taking my health. You are not taking my husband. You are not taking my wife. You are not taking my kids. These are mine, and I am defending them in the name of Jesus, and God is going to give me a great victory!"

**Rise up with the fire of God in your eyes,
His Word in your mouth and His power in your hands,
and defeat the devil. Stop being passive.**

What made these men mighty? They were pushed too far and got fed up. The minute they started getting aggressive, the anointing of God came on them and they were able to do supernatural things. Nothing's changed today. You can be just as aggressive. You can defend your stuff and take back what the devil stole from you. You can rise up with the fire of God in your eyes, His Word in your mouth and His power in your hands, and defeat the devil. Stop being passive. Start being aggressive.

Some time ago, my wife and I were being spiritually attacked from every angle. This or that would break, something else would stop working, and other things kept falling apart. At one point, we were almost at each other's throats, bickering like nothing we've ever experienced before. We were incredibly drained by these attacks. One day we both left the office and were going to have lunch somewhere. We walked into a restaurant where we were told we had to wait 45 minutes. Neither of us wanted to wait, so we went back outside to decide on another place to eat.

We hadn't been in that restaurant more than 10 minutes when we got back outside and saw that the wire wheel hubcaps were missing off our car! Someone had stolen them within that tiny space of time. Now that was the second time in two weeks we had experienced this. My wife just about came undone. It was the straw that broke the camel's back. Boy, the fire of God came over her and she took authority over the devil, and I joined right in with her. We got fed up!

I want you to know that by sunset that day everything that had been stolen from us had been returned to us. That night, I realized that we could have had the victory earlier in the week instead of going through all the harassment if we had gotten more aggressive. We all have times when we become passive. Instead of getting fed up, we tolerate things and just roll with the punches. But we can't win that way. We need to be sober and vigilant. We need to be on guard. We need to refuse to listen to the devil's enchanting whispers. Don't let the devil get you off in a corner somewhere and start deceiving you with his flavored words. Don't let him convince you that nobody understands what you're going through and, even if they did, wouldn't care. The only way to break the yoke off of your neck is to get fed up, take your sword and launch an attack.

Fight Fear—Develop the Attitude of Faith and Be Steadfast

In the book of Deuteronomy, God revealed to the nation of Israel a proper attitude for engaging in warfare with the adversary. "When you go out to fight your enemies and you face horses and chariots and an army greater than your own, do not be afraid. The LORD your God, who brought you out of the land of Egypt, is with you!" (Deut. 20:1-2, *NLT*).

Did you notice that God is already warning the Israelites of the strong possibility that they might be outnumbered, that the situation they would face might seem impossible? Have you ever been there before? Do you regularly face impossible situations? This is a normal part of spiritual warfare. But what God is reminding us is that in the midst of these battles—"Do not be afraid." What this verse tells me is that fear is a favorable position as far as Satan is concerned. It is a disadvantage for us to operate in fear because it means we are operating in the opposite force of faith. Fear brings Satan on the scene. Faith brings God on the scene.

Faith and fear are opposite forces. They arrive the same way but from different sources. "So then faith cometh by hearing, and hearing by the word of God" (Rom. 10:17, *KJV*). So then *fear* comes by hearing, and hearing by the word of the devil. Faith is not a mental force; it is a spiritual force that comes to the heart. Fear is not a mental force, but a spiritual force. It can affect the mind just like faith can. When you have faith in your heart, it will affect your attitude. In the same way, if you have fear in your heart, it will affect your attitude. Faith and fear are also released the same way: by words and by actions.

Satan knows that if he can create enough pressure on you from negative circumstances—if he can make it look as though the odds against your winning are a million to one—then chances are you will begin to fear, and that automatically puts him in a favorable position. He really cannot bring anything to pass in your life unless you first give him legal right. You give him legal right through fear. You might be thinking, *Well wait a minute, brother*

Jerry, you don't know what I'm going through. I have a right to be afraid. Sure you have a right to be afraid; you just don't have the right to stay afraid unless you want to be defeated. I am not telling you that I never have opportunities to be fearful. I have to cast down fear and resist it just like you do, because every day of my life I face things that seem impossible.

Fear brings Satan on the scene.
Faith brings God on the scene.

We have to stop being so afraid. More importantly, we have to stop panicking; because when we panic, we throw all spiritual logic out the window. I don't care how long you've been a Christian or have been going to church; how many sermon CDs you listen to; how many books you read; how many spiritual seminars you attend. When you panic, you forget everything you ever learned about spiritual warfare. Instead of leaning on God, you lean on your own understanding and give Satan the upper hand.

There are two reasons in this verse why we shouldn't fear. The first is because *God is with us*. Unfortunately, that sometimes doesn't have the impact on our lives that it should. If that means nothing more to you than a Pentecostal cliché, you are in trouble. It reminds me of what I overheard once when I first went into the ministry. I was preaching in a little full gospel church in Arkansas. During the course of my sermon, I made the statement, "I live by faith. God is my source." I said this boldly, even though I was a little young in the Lord.

Wouldn't you know, at the end of the service, as I was walking out the lobby of the church, I heard two elderly women talking about me. One said to the other, "Did you hear what he said?" The other woman replied, "Yes, I did. He said he lives by faith." And the other lady said, "Poor thing . . . nobody to trust but God." And just like good ol' Southern folk are accustomed to saying, she ended the conversation with, "Awe, bless his heart." Can you imagine? Feeling sorry for me because I had nobody to trust but God? Who else do you need?! Don't feel sorry for me when I say I live by faith. Feel sorry for the person who doesn't know how to.

The second reason God told His people not to fear is because He had already brought them up out of the land of Egypt. God was saying, "Look, I delivered you once before, and I can do it again. I saved you out of that impossible situation in Egypt, and I can deliver you out of this impossible situation today."

The devil hopes you'll forget all your past victories and miracles. He hopes that you'll get tunnel vision and all you'll see is the new problem in front of you that has "impossible" written all over it. If you bring your victories to his attention, then there's a strong possibility he'll flee, because that's one of his weaknesses. He cannot stand hearing about his defeats.

If you've ever been healed before, you can be healed again. If you've ever had a financial miracle before, you can have one again. If God has ever delivered you before, He can come through for you again. Don't forget the last impossible thing that God got you out of; He can do it again! Don't fear. Don't panic. Don't give Satan the favorable position he needs to defeat you.

The book of Psalms warns us to not be like some of the people of Israel, who were "a stubborn and rebellious generation; a generation that set not their heart aright, and whose spirit was not steadfast with God" (Ps. 78:8, *KJV*). Think about these words: "whose spirit was not steadfast with God." These people were a compromising people. They gave up under pressure. They gave up at the very slightest sight of defeat. They were not steadfast.

If you do not develop a steadfast spirit, Satan knows that he can get you to compromise under pressure. He will keep attacking that one particular area of weakness to gain a favorable position. If he gets you to compromise once, he'll make a record of what it actually took for you to compromise. And he'll start at that same place again. He knows that if you gave in before, then it won't take as much effort from him the second time around.

After the writer of this psalm tells us about the rebellious generation whose spirit was not steadfast with God, he gives us an example in the following verse: "The children of Ephraim, being armed, and carrying bows, turned back in the day of battle" (Ps. 78:9, *KJV*). These guys were armed and dangerous. They were well equipped to win the battle, yet they allowed what they saw of the enemy to convince them there was no way to defeat them. So they dropped their weapons and fled.

This is exactly what happens to a lot of Christians. Satan has only one weapon—deception. He can break it down into other forms, but it's his mightiest weapon. It's all he's really got. On the contrary, we, as believers, have multiple weapons through God that are able to pull down strongholds. We simply have more power than the devil does. Because the enemy does not have the arsenal to beat you, what does he have to do to win? He has to convince you to drop your weapon. He'll have to be a good talker. He'll have to use some very deceptive words to convince you that you can't win.

I remember something that happened to me once as a boy. Every time I think about this, a part of me laughs, because I realize how stupid kids can be. I grew up with a boy named Johnny who was the same age as me and lived one block away. His parents owned a big vacant lot next to their house, and a bunch of us would go over there after school and play football. One day, my best friend, Kenny, and I were playing football with Johnny. For some reason, Kenny and I didn't like Johnny very much. So on this one day, we decided to give this poor fellow a hard time. Kenny and I plotted and planned that every time this kid had the ball, we were going to gang tackle him. We were going to hurt him just because we didn't like him, even though it was Johnny's ball we were playing with and Johnny's property we were playing on.

One day, Johnny got mad. He got so mad he ran inside his house, came back with a shotgun and pointed the thing at Kenny. Man, I'll never forget this as long as I live. I stood right next to Kenny and watched Johnny shove that gun in his face while he was crying and yelling, "I'm going to kill you. I'm going to blow your head off." Kenny didn't bat an eyelash. He reached up and stuck his finger in the barrel of that gun and told Johnny, "I'm not kidding you. If you pull that trigger, I'm gonna break your neck." He started talking Johnny into dropping the gun. Minutes later, Johnny did just that. He dropped the gun, started crying again and begged Kenny not to break his neck. It never dawned on Johnny that if he pulled the trigger, nobody was going to be breaking any-body's neck. Kenny managed to convince Johnny to drop his weapon out of fear.

The devil does to us what Kenny did to Johnny. Here we are with the armor of God, the powerful name of Jesus, the Holy Spirit and angelic beings at our disposal, and the devil comes up to us and threatens us by saying, "I'm gonna take everything you've got." And we drop all our weapons and act like heaven doesn't exist, like the name of Jesus is no more powerful than any other name, and we run away. Why? Because we are afraid.

Yet God has already equipped us to win. There is no excuse for us being defeated. Our adversary is already a defeated foe. Jesus has already beaten him—at Calvary. If we allow fear to overtake us, then we are letting someone who has already been defeated talk us into dropping our weapons. That's not very smart.

Let me tell you something. The storms you may be experiencing in your life right now could very well be at their end. The eye of the hurricane could have already passed over you. But Satan is going to keep throwing up smoke screens and thunder and lightning and all kinds of things to make you think this is going to be with you forever. He's going to do whatever he needs to do to cause you to panic. Don't be like the people who did not have a steadfast spirit, who did not set their hearts right and gave up in the day of battle. Remember, the Lord has gotten you out of seemingly impossible situations before, and He'll get you out again. Don't give the devil a favorable position. Do not fear, because God is on your side.

5

THE SHADOW OF A DOG NEVER BIT ANYONE

Shadows and Smokescreens

I received one of my greatest revelations from brother Kenneth Copeland when he came to preach in my hometown of Shreveport, Louisiana, in 1969. I was running from God then. I knew I was called to preach, but I didn't want to. When brother Copeland came, my wife begged me every day to go hear him speak. Finally, on his last night there, to keep Carolyn quiet, I told her, "I'll go on one condition. We'll sit on the back row closest to the exit, and when he starts telling all those tear-jerking stories and begging for money, that's when I'm leaving, and you can get home the best way you can. Is that a deal?" Carolyn said, "That's a deal!"

So we went, and I sat on the back pew prepared not to believe anything this preacher said. I'll never forget what happened after the worship leader sang the last song right before they turned over the service to brother Copeland. He walked up to the platform, took his Bible and firmly set it on the podium. Then he said, "Don't ever sing that song again in my presence. It is embalmed with unbelief!" At that moment, I became a defender of the faith. It made me mad. I thought to myself, *Who does he think he is? We can sing whatever we want to in our church.* Suddenly, it became *my* church. From that point on, I was on the edge of my chair, listening to every word brother Copeland said, which was exactly how God planned to get my attention.

As I walked away that night, God became real to me. Jesus was no longer in the same category as Santa Claus or the Easter Bunny. The Bible was no longer just a storybook or a history book. In one service, my life was changed. Later, I gave my life to the Lord.

I wanted to know God. I wanted to know Jesus. I wanted to know the Holy Spirit. Eventually, the Lord spoke to me and said, "Now shut your business down and treat the Word like it's your business. You spend the next three months in your bedroom, no less than eight hours a day, studying My Word; and when you come out of there, I'll make a preacher out of you."

I listened to tapes of brother Copeland from one end to the other. I dissected them. I fed on them. I almost wore them slick. While I was studying the Word, I had a lot of questions. But for some reason, no one was able to answer them for me. I figured if I could just have the opportunity to ask brother Copeland, I would find my answers. I was given that opportunity when he came back to our town. You can imagine my surprise when he told me, "Jerry, the Lord showed me that you've got some questions that you need answered. What are they?" I was so shocked I couldn't even remember my name, much less my list of questions.

Finally I said, "Brother Copeland, I have no problem believing God for healing. In fact, I'm walking in divine health. My family is walking in divine health. But would you please tell me how to talk God into meeting my financial needs?" He looked at me and said, "God's already done everything He's going to do about your finances."

I said, "You're kidding me! Please tell me that He's not going to leave me in the mess I'm in." Brother Copeland replied, "That isn't what I'm talking about." Then he shared something with me that made absolutely no sense whatsoever. He said, "Jerry, the shadow of a dog never bit anyone." And then he walked away!

That was the revelation I'd been waiting to hear?! I thought that was the craziest thing I had ever heard in my life. I had no idea what he meant, and he left me to figure it out for myself.

**Satan's tactic is to intercept the light
coming from the Word of God in order to cast a shadow
on it before its light can reach our minds and spirits.
He does this so we will be controlled by fear.**

As crazy as it sounded, I could not get that statement out of my head. I thought about it day and night, night and day. *The shadow of a dog never bit anyone.* The word "shadow" kept popping out at me, so I thought about it some more and slowly started getting somewhere. The only Scripture I could think of that even mentioned the word shadow was in Psalm 23:4: "Yea, though I walk through the valley of the shadow of death, I will fear no evil" (*KJV*).

So I started to meditate on that verse. I read it over and over and over, but I still couldn't figure out what it meant. Yet I knew there had to be something in that verse that had to do with what brother Copeland told me. I began to read it slowly, word by word. "Yea, though I walk through the valley of the *shadow* of death, I will fear no evil." Finally it clicked. The verse didn't read, "Yea, though I walk through the valley of death." It was talking about the valley of the *shadow* of death. There's a difference. The valley of the shadow of death doesn't mean that death is inevitable.

I dug in further. I looked up the definition of the word "shadow," which means "a definite area of shade cast upon a surface by a body intercepting light rays; the dark image made by such a body." When I read that, here's how I applied it. Satan's tactic is to intercept the light coming from the Word of God in order to cast a dark image, or shadow, on it before its light can reach our minds and spirits. He does this so that we will be controlled by fear. Shadows are simply smokescreens used by Satan. He engineers them to leave a false impression on our minds. When brother Copeland told me, "The shadow of a dog never bit anyone," he was saying, "Jerry, you're dealing with shadows. The devil is trying to convince you that your financial needs will never be met. It's nothing but a shadow, and shadows can't hurt you. Dogs bite, but their shadows don't."

Have you ever made shadowy figures with your hand using a projector? You know what I'm talking about. You put your fingers up in the air and move them around so that they resemble all sorts of animals and things on the screen. Not too long ago, I did this while I was playing around with my grandsons. I made my fingers transform on the screen into the shape of a rabbit. The boys went nuts. "PaPa," they cried. "There's a rabbit on the screen! Where did it come from? Wow!" Of course I was leading them on. The shadows weren't real rabbits; they were false impressions. My grandsons, though, were totally convinced they were real until I showed them how I was doing it.

The devil does the same thing. He casts shadows, false impressions of things, on our lives all the time. He stands in the corner making all sorts of signs that you might imagine are real. Shadows are intended by Satan to cause you to fear, give up and quit.

Another example of this is found in Matthew 14. The disciples were in a terrible storm on the water when Jesus came out to meet them:

> When the disciples saw him, they screamed in terror, thinking he was a ghost. But Jesus spoke to them at once. "It's all right," he said. "I am here! Don't be afraid." Then Peter called to him, "Lord, if it's really you, tell me to come to you by walking on the water." "All right, come," Jesus said. So Peter went over the side of the boat and walked on the water toward Jesus. But when he looked around at the high waves, he was terrified and began to sink. "Save me, Lord!" he shouted. Instantly Jesus reached out his hand and grabbed him. "You don't have much faith," Jesus said. "Why did you doubt me?" (Matt. 14:26-31, *NLT*).

Notice that Peter was a success as long as he kept his eyes on Jesus. But when he saw the strong wind, he became afraid. What was the wind? A shadow. What was it attempting to do? Intercept the light rays from Jesus' words—"Come"—to Peter. It cast a dark shadow between Peter and his destiny. It created fear in his heart, so he started to sink. What has wind got to do with walking on water? Is there some law that says you can't walk on the water when it's windy? Of course not.

So how do we stop Satan from intercepting the light from God's Word? Simple. We have to stay focused. The devil will do whatever it takes to keep you out of the Word. He'll put television between you and the Word. He'll put the *USA Today* between you and the Word. He'll put the evening news between you and the Word. He'll put a sincere but sincerely wrong Christian between you and the Word. Keeping you from the Word keeps fear in your life, and that is what Satan wants to do.

Satan has already been defeated.
When you stand up to him with the Word of God,
he runs away in stark terror.

When you get full of the Word of God, you find out a few things. You find out that you are the one with the weapons that are mighty through God to the pulling down of strongholds. You find out that you're the one with the authority. You're the one with the power. You find out that Satan has already been defeated. And when you stand up to him with the Word of God in your mouth and command him to flee, he runs away in what the *Amplified Bible* says: stark terror. But if the devil can cast a dark shadow over some area of your life, then he can cause you to lose the will to even put up a fight.

A shadow is also defined as something without reality or substance. In other words, the wind that terrified Peter had no substance, yet he gave into it and began to sink. Now, I know you might be thinking, *Wait a minute, brother Jerry. You said that shadows have no substance, that they are not real. But sickness is very real.* I'm not denying the reality of sickness. I'm acknowledging a higher form of reality. Jesus said, "Thy Word is truth" (John 17:17, *KJV*). The dictionary definition for truth is "the highest form of reality that exists." Yes, sickness is real. Financial problems are real. Stress is real. Depression is real. But the Truth is a higher form of reality. When you apply a higher form of reality to a lower form, all things being equal, then the lower form must bow.

I don't live in a fantasy world. I live in faith. I live in the Word. I live in the highest form of reality that exists. When problems come, I don't say, "This is not really a problem." No, I say, "Hold it right there, problem. Let's see what the Word says about you." Whatever you are going through today is not the highest form of reality. Shadows are not the truth. But Satan wants you to think they are.

No matter what shadows the devil casts at you, if you hold on to God and His Word, they will get you out of trouble. That is God's promise. If you allow Satan's shadows to darken you, then you lose sight of that promise. You are not remembering your covenant. God says, "Trust me! I won't let you down." Satan says, "What if God doesn't show up?" "What if it doesn't work?" "What if God forgets?" "What if it doesn't happen?" The best way to get rid of the devil is to talk back to him with God's Word. He has no defense against the Word of God.

When I first left brother Copeland's organization and Carolyn and I launched out into our own ministry, we hit the ground running! I guess I had been in my own ministry about two years when we experienced a mountain of financial problems. The devil knocked the props right out from under us. Up to this point, we hadn't struggled financially. Our ministry was young, but it was flourishing. But then things started looking pretty bad. Suddenly, it seemed like our whole ministry was going to come crashing down.

As I was in my bedroom praying about this, fear kept trying to rise up on the inside of me. The devil told me, "You failed in your business, and you're going to fail in your ministry. You always get up to this point and then you hit rock bottom. You did it in business and you're going to do it in ministry." Fear tried to grip me through these negative thoughts, but I knew enough about the Word to cast down those imaginations. Wouldn't you know it, as soon as I would cast them down, they would come back again. So I kept on rebuking them, and I kept praying in the Holy Spirit, but I kept hearing the devil calling me a failure. "You're a failure! This is as far as you're going to go. I'm going to take everything you've got." He kept going on and on and on. But at some point, he called me a failure one too many times.

Suddenly coming out of me was this righteous indignation, and I knew it wasn't just my voice but the voice of the Holy Spirit. I heard the Holy Spirit say, "You want to talk about failure, let's talk about you, Satan!" The Holy Spirit, through me, started telling the devil how he got kicked out of heaven; how he was defeated at the Cross; and how he was stripped of the keys of death, hell and the grave. Then—I'll never forget this—I said, "Now, Satan. We've talked about failure. Now let's talk about your future. That ain't too bright either. You're headed for the Lake of Fire. And guess where Jerry's headed? He's headed for victory! He's headed for glory! He's headed for the presence of Almighty God!"

I came out of that room with a shout in my heart. And let me tell you what, God met my financial need during that season, and He's been doing it ever since. All that trash the devil was telling me was a shadow. All he's got are shadows—the shadow of death; the shadow of defeat; the shadow of failure; the shadow of fear.

**The next time Satan tries to discourage you,
let him know that his threats are nothing but a shadow,
which cannot hurt you.**

Let's look at another example found in Mark 5. Here we have a story of a man by the name of Jairus, who was a ruler of the synagogue:

After Jesus crossed over by boat, a large crowd met him at the seaside. One of the meeting-place leaders named Jairus came. When he saw Jesus, he fell to his knees, beside himself as he begged, "My dear daughter is at death's door. Come and lay hands on her so she will get well and live." Jesus went with him, the whole crowd tagging along, pushing and jostling him. . . . While he [Jesus] was still talking, some people came from the leader's house and told him, "Your daughter is dead. Why bother the Teacher any more?" Jesus overheard what they were talking about and said to the leader, "Don't listen to them; just trust me."

He permitted no one to go in with him except Peter, James, and John. They entered the leader's house and pushed their way through the gossips looking for a story and neighbors bringing in casseroles. Jesus was abrupt: "Why all this busybody grief and gossip? This child isn't dead; she's sleeping." Provoked to sarcasm, they told him he didn't know what he was talking about. But when he had sent them all out, he took the child's father and mother, along with his companions, and entered the child's room. He clasped the girl's hand and said, "Talitha koum," which means, "Little girl, get up." At that, she was up and walking around! This girl was twelve years of age. They, of course, were all beside themselves with joy. He gave them strict orders that no one was to know what had taken place in that room. Then he said, "Give her something to eat" (Mark 5:21-24,35-43, *THE MESSAGE*).

That's a very simple story, and yet it can make a powerful impact in your life if you will listen to it closely. Jesus was saying that what those people had said to Jairus was nothing but shadows. He said that when shadows come into your life—when you're believing for one thing and a different report comes in its stead—we must continue to trust in Him. If you keep listening to negative reports, the shadows get darker and darker, and it affects your imagination and your thoughts. It gets between you and the Word. You're not looking to Jesus, and you begin to lose your focus and your faith. Now you're fearful, and fear attracts Satan like faith attracts God.

If you give God's Word first place in your life, then God confirms His Word with signs following. If you join with Satan, then

Satan has legal right to confirm his word with signs following. Have you ever noticed how Satan will keep trying to get you to go for his lies? You can wake up in the morning and have a pain in your side or in your arm, and the devil will immediately say, "Arthritis." You might respond by saying, "No, that's not arthritis." And he'll come back with, "Bursitis?" You might say, "Nope, this is not bursitis." And he'll start naming off ailments like heart attack and stroke just to see what you'll fall for. All he's doing is casting shadows at you.

Remember what Jesus said about the man whose daughter some said was dead? He didn't say, "Did they say *dead*? Dead? Oh, dear God. Get me out of here quick. I've healed a few headaches, but I don't know about death." No. It didn't frighten Him in the least. He turned and told Jairus, "Don't listen to them, and let's go." Sometimes before you can get anything done, you have to first get rid of all the unbelief. Get rid of all the religious people. All the doubters. All the naysayers. Finally, Jesus said to the little girl, "Daughter, arise." What that means is, "Little lamb, it's time to wake up." Death was but a shadow.

There are shadows in your life today that have no substance. Satan is trying to get you to buy into them. He's telling you, "Oh, you're going under this year. Business is going to be bad and you're not going to make it. You're going to lose everything you've got." Just know that you don't have to accept those lies. Stay with God's Word and just watch what God will do.

I want to encourage you the way brother Copeland encouraged me. Whatever you are facing, you are not alone. Jesus is by your side. You may have been told, "There's not enough money." That's a shadow. You may have been told, "You'll never be healed of that disease!" That's a shadow. You may have been told, "Your kids will never get off drugs." That's a shadow. The next time Satan tries to discourage you with a lack of finances, sickness or family problems, let him know from the start that his threats are nothing but a shadow, and shadows cannot hurt you.

6

LOOKS LIKE A JOB FOR EL SHADDAI

"With men this is impossible; but with God all things are possible" (Matt. 19:26, *KJV*). " 'What do you mean, "If I can"?' Jesus asked. 'Anything is possible if a person believes'" (Mark 9:23, *NLT*). Whenever a problem—or what someone might call impossibility—arises in my life, I don't declare it impossible. I just smile real big and say, "Looks like another challenge for the Word of God." What looks to be impossible is just another opportunity for you to turn a test into a testimony.

Let me share with you a story about a situation that looked impossible for a man named Abraham and his wife, Sarah. It comes out of the Old Testament:

> Abraham and Sarah were already old and well advanced in years, and Sarah was long past the age of childbearing. So Sarah laughed to herself as she thought, "After I am worn out and my master is old, will I now have this pleasure?" Then the Lord said to Abraham, "Why did Sarah laugh and say, 'Will I really have a child, now that I am old?' Is anything too hard for the Lord? I will return to you at the appointed time next year and Sarah will have a son" (Gen. 18:11-14, *NIV*).

Now let's go back a few chapters earlier and pick up on a conversation that had taken place many years before:

> Abram replied, "O Sovereign Lord, what good are all your blessings when I don't even have a son? Since I don't have

a son, Eliezer of Damascus, a servant in my household, will inherit all my wealth. You have given me no children, so one of my servants will be my heir." Then the LORD said to him, "No, your servant will not be your heir, for you will have a son of your own to inherit everything I am giving you." Then the LORD brought Abram outside beneath the night sky and told him, "Look up into the heavens and count the stars if you can. Your descendants will be like that—too many to count!" And Abram believed the LORD, and the LORD declared him righteous because of his faith (Gen. 15:2-6, *NLT*).

It's important to notice that God told Abraham he would have a child who would be his heir; the son he already had was not the heir. If you are familiar with this story, you know that Sarah was unable to conceive. The Bible tells us that her womb was dead. But God told Abraham that he would have a son from his barren wife. Abraham and Sarah both thought it was impossible. It could never happen. There was absolutely no way. It violated natural laws. Nevertheless, God had spoken something over them supernaturally that was impossible in the natural.

I like what I heard Gloria Copeland say one time. She said, "God has never told Kenneth and me to do anything that was possible. If it were possible, then it would not take faith. And it's impossible to please God without faith." You might say that if everything you do is possible in the natural, then it just may be that you haven't heard from God yet.

Everything God tells us to do is impossible in the natural because He requires our faith. If you can accomplish everything in your own might, with your own resources and in your own ability, intellect and wisdom, then you need to question whether or not you are doing what God wants you to do. If you can do it, then what do you need Him for? God wants you involved in things that, in the natural, you cannot do. Boy, when He called me, He found somebody who couldn't do anything. This is what makes me say that without Him I am nothing, but in Him I am unlimited. "I can do all things through Christ which strengtheneth me" (Phil. 4:13, *KJV*).

It May Be . . . or It May Not

Abraham and Sarah were faced with an impossible situation. They could not produce what God was asking them to produce, so they decided to take matters into their own hands. Sarah, Abraham's wife, had not been able to bear children for him. But she had an Egyptian servant named Hagar. So Sarah said to Abraham, "The LORD has kept me from having children. . . . Go and sleep with my servant. Perhaps I can have children through her" (Gen. 16:2, *NLT*). The *King James Version* quotes Sarah as having said to her husband, "I pray thee, go in unto my maid; *it may be* that I may obtain children by her" (emphasis added).

Let me give you a warning. Any time you start dealing with "it may be," you are about to lean into the arm of the flesh. Remember, God is always exact. There are no "it may be's" with God. I remember the first time I got involved in an "it may be." I had surrendered my life to the Lord and accepted my call to preach. I was learning to live by faith the way I heard it preached by brother Kenneth Copeland. At the time, I felt that God was going to call me to a traveling ministry. Well, you've got to have a means of transportation to do that. If you're going to be a mobile ministry, then you need something to get from point A to point B.

I had a problem in my life. My "something" was broke. It was a 1964 Oldsmobile Luxury Sedan that luxury had left many years ago. I paid $187.50 for it, and the odometer had turned over more than 100,000 miles. That old car was absolutely worn out. Actually, it was a total wreck when I bought it. The original owner ran it into a tree, so I did a lot of rebuilding on it. By the time I got through with it, it looked good. You really couldn't tell it had ever been wrecked. But still, the engine was on its way out along with the transmission.

I knew I was going to be a traveling preacher, but my means of transportation was shot. I thought, *I'm just going to live by faith.* I figured if I was going to believe for a car, then I needed to check out a few. I went to all the dealerships. I had worked in many of those dealerships, so the folks at those places knew me well. I picked up new car brochures, brought them home and laid them on the floor in a circle. I got right down in the middle of that pile of brochures and started praying in the Spirit. Surely, God would lead me and place my hand on the car that He wanted me to have. So I prayed for a while and determined that God wanted me to have something in the way of a station wagon; with a wife and two kids, we would need plenty of space.

One day, I came up to my wife and told her to put on her Sunday best. We went to the new car dealership that sold the particular car I believed God wanted me to have and asked one of the salesmen if we could take a look at it. We took it for a test drive, and did we fall in love with that car! The salesman came back and asked us what we thought of it. "That's the one we want, all right," I replied. "Great," he said. "Come into my office."

The guy began to get his paperwork together, and I began to get a little nervous. See, I didn't have a dime to my name. I was believing that God was going to show up. I was thinking, *Surely, it may be.* We started going through the basic questions on the forms and then he asked, "So, how do you plan to pay for this car?"

**Any time you start dealing with "it may be,"
you are about to lean into the arm of the flesh.
There are no "it may be's" with God.**

I looked at him for a moment and said, "My Father's going to buy it for me." "Oh, really?" the man asked. "How will your father finance this?" "He's going to pay cash," I replied. He then asked me what my father did. "Oh, He does a lot of stuff. You name it; He does it. I mean, you know, He's just into a lot of things." I started feeling under pressure. I kept looking around to see if some angel was going to fly right into the dealership with a bag full of money and drop it on the table.

I mean, it *may* be. The problem was that God had not orchestrated any of this. This was all Jerry. Not God, but Jerry. I continued to sit in that office where the salesman continued to ask me questions that kept boxing me in. Finally, I broke. I told him, "Sir, forgive me. I apologize. You're going to think I'm a fool, but I've got to tell you what happened. I surrendered my life to the Lord, and right now I'm endeavoring to live by faith. I thought that somehow God would meet me in some way and buy me this car. I apologize for wasting your time. I've made a fool of myself and I've embarrassed my family."

The salesman looked at me and said, "You're a Christian." "Yes," I replied. "Give me your hand," he said. He then took my hand and said, "Father, I agree in the name of Jesus." That made me feel a little better, but God never showed up, and I walked out of the dealership without a car. I realized that I had, like Abraham and Sarah, taken things into my own hands. I believed, "Surely, God wanted this car for me." But I was not being led by God; I was being led by myself. You've got to be careful of thinking, "Surely, it *may* be."

The Problem with Ishmaels

Now, Sarah apparently thought this way as well, because she was faced with an impossible situation. God told her and her husband that she would have a child even though it was physically impossible. So Sarah, in her own mind, tried to figure out how it was going to happen. The story, as you read a little of it earlier, goes on to tell us that Abraham came in one day from doing whatever it was he was doing, and the conversation went something like this.

"Hi, Sarah," Abraham said. "Hello, Abraham," she replied. "You know, I've been praying all day. I've been meditating on what God told us about this child business. You know it's impossible for me to conceive, and while I believe God wants us to have a child, I think what He really meant was that you need to have it through my house maiden, Hagar. She's the one who can conceive. *It may be* . . . now listen to me, Abraham, *it may be* this is the way God intended for this to come to pass. You pray about it and let me know what you think. Take your time." Abraham didn't need much time. He looked at his wife and said, "That's a wonderful idea." He didn't even pray about it. "Yep. Sounds like God to me."

What happened is that Abraham and Hagar eventually got together. Hagar conceived and they named their baby boy Ishmael. At the time, Abraham was 86 years old. The next chapter in Genesis begins with, "When Abram was 99 years old, the Lord appeared to him and said, 'I am God Almighty; serve me faithfully and live a blameless life. I will make a covenant with you, by which I will guarantee to make you into a mighty nation'" (Gen. 17:1-2, *NLT*).

After Ishmael was born, the next time God spoke to Abraham was 13 years later. There were 13 years of silence between the two of them. Why? Because Ishmael was not God's will. Ishmael was a result of Abraham leaning to the arm of the flesh. The book of Galatians tells us that Ishmael was born after the flesh and Isaac (the son who would be miraculously born to Sarah and Abraham) was born by promise (see Gal. 4:23). In other words, there are things you can produce out of the flesh and there are things that can be produced by standing on the promises of God.

I don't know about you, but I've had some "Ishmaels" in my life (I call the things that we make happen because of our lack of patience "Ishmaels"). I used to think I had better ideas than God because He was taking too long to fulfill His promises. I remember one time when I had sold my airplane and, by the instruction of the Lord, I split the money between two different ministries. I still needed an airplane—my schedule demanded it—but I was stuck without an airplane. So I began believing God for another airplane. You would think that after I had given this money away the other airplane would have shown up the next day. I needed it the next day, after all. But it didn't show up. It didn't show up in a week. It didn't show up in a month. It didn't even show up in a year.

One day, out of the blue, a man called and told me he had an airplane to sell me, a "Jim Dandy" little airplane. He invited me out to Meacham Airport to take a look at it. That was the first thing I'd heard in a long time about airplanes, and I was quite desperate at that point. So I met him and looked at it closely. Honestly, I wanted an airplane so badly that I wouldn't have cared if it were a lawn mower with wings. I looked at the airplane, and it looked back at me like it wanted me to own it.

Keep in mind that God had told me years before, "I will keep you in airplanes in your ministry, but you are never to borrow money for them. I don't want you flying an airplane with money owed against it." I didn't have money to buy that airplane, but the guy who wanted to sell it told me, "I've been praying." He wanted to sell it to me at wholesale—below market value. Well, it sounded like God to me! The problem was the guy wanted to sell it quickly.

He didn't have long to wait; he needed an immediate decision.

I asked God, "Is this You?" I never got an answer because I knew it wasn't God. Why? Because I didn't have the money to pay for it. But I wanted it so badly that I borrowed the money to get it. It wasn't a lot, but I had the most difficult and painful time making that payment each month. I asked God what the problem was and He told me, "You're flying an Ishmael. You leaned to the arm of the flesh. You didn't stand on My promise; so what you have produced is an Ishmael." I didn't know what to do about it, so I asked Him. God told me to believe Him for the money to pay it off and then give it away to someone He already had in mind.

Ishmael was a result of Abraham leaning to the flesh.
Ishmael was born after the flesh, and Isaac was born by promise.
There are things you can produce out of the flesh and there are things
that can be produced by standing on the promises of God.

You know what? When I made that agreement with God, the money came quickly and I paid off the debt. One day I was having a meeting in Fort Worth, and I invited the man to whom God had told me to give the plane as one of my guest speakers. But I was a little confused. I said to God, "If I give this airplane to that man, then he's going to have an Ishmael, too." God replied, "No, he won't. He's believing for it debt free. It will be an Isaac for him." That man was Happy Caldwell. Right before he started to speak, I handed him the keys to the plane. He was so thrilled, and the plane was a blessing to his life.

That's the last time I ever flew an Ishmael. I don't drive Ishmael cars. I don't wear Ishmael clothes. I don't live in Ishmael houses. I don't have an Ishmael ministry. Ishmael was not a product of faith. Ishmael was a compromise.

When El Shaddai Shows Up

Let's take a look at a passage from the book of Romans and get a description of Abraham and his faith as written by Paul:

That's why faith is the key! God's promise is given to us as a free gift. And we are certain to receive it, whether or not we follow Jewish customs, if we have faith like Abraham's. For Abraham is the father of all who believe. That is what the Scriptures mean when God told him, "I have made you the father of many nations." This happened because Abraham believed in the God who brings the dead back to life and who brings into existence what didn't exist before. When God promised Abraham that he would become the father of many nations, Abraham believed him. God had also said, "Your descendants will be as numerous as the stars," even though such a promise seemed utterly impossible! And Abraham's faith did not weaken, even though he knew that he was too old to be a father at the age of one hundred and that Sarah, his wife, had never been able to have children. Abraham never wavered in believing God's promise. In fact, his faith grew stronger, and in this he brought glory to God. He was absolutely convinced that God was able to do anything he promised. And because of Abraham's faith, God declared him to be righteous (Rom. 4:16-22, *NLT*).

Abraham's giving in to his wife's suggestion that he conceive a child with her handmaiden certainly doesn't sound like the man Paul described here. Why doesn't it say in Genesis that after Sarah said he should mate with another woman, Abraham said something back to her like this: "In the name of Almighty God, I rebuke that thought. I am not weakening my faith in the promise of God. I consider not my body or the deadness of your womb. We're going to stand on God's Word. Now, Sarah, I don't know what you've been doing all day, girl, but it's not praying. You need to quit watching those soap operas because something got down on the inside of you that isn't God."

That's not what Abraham said, of course. So something here is not making sense. Are we talking about the same man of faith in Romans as the one we read about in Genesis? What was Paul talking about when he said, "Abraham's faith did not weaken" and "Abraham never wavered in believing God's promise"? What Paul wrote was a description of Abraham not when he was 75 or 85 years old. It's a description of Abraham when he was 99 years old. Something happened to him at that age that changed his life forever. From that moment on, he never staggered at the promise of God again.

So what happened? Read the verse in Genesis again. "When Abraham was ninety-nine years old, the LORD appeared to him and said, 'I am God Almighty; serve me faithfully and live a blameless life' " (Gen. 17:1, *NLT*). At the age of 99, Abraham had a visitation from El Shaddai. You may be wondering what the big deal is. You have to understand that prior to that time, Abraham did not know God as "El Shaddai." He knew God as "Elohim," which in the Hebrew means "the God who created heaven and earth," "the God who created nature" and "the God who created all natural laws."

The reason Sarah had a hard time with God telling her she was going to bear a child was because in her mind that violated the laws of Elohim. Elohim created man. Elohim created woman. Elohim created the reproductive organs. Elohim created the laws of reproduction. And in the laws that Elohim created concerning reproduction, you must have a sperm, an egg and a womb that is able to conceive. But since she couldn't conceive, Abraham and Sarah compromised. They hatched their own plan.

Thirteen years later, God appeared to Abraham, but not only as Elohim, creator or preserver of natural law. He appeared as El Shaddai, which means "the One who reserves the right to reverse, override, prolong or accelerate natural laws." God told Abraham, "I am appearing to you today as El Shaddai, and I reserve the right to override natural laws." Once Abraham got hold of that, he didn't waver in his faith. He stood strong. He didn't consider his dead body or the barren womb of his wife any longer. He began preparing for the arrival of his son Isaac, the son born of promise.

It takes El Shaddai coming on the scene when you're faced with a situation that looks impossible. When things can't happen in the natural, it's a job for El Shaddai. Paul wrote, "Whereas the child [Ishmael] of the slave woman was born according to the flesh and had an ordinary birth" (Gal. 4:23, *AMP*). That's the reason Ishmael could never be the heir, the seed, to Abraham's promise. He came by ordinary birth. God did not want Isaac, the promised son, coming by ordinary means. He wanted Isaac coming by supernatural means. He wanted El Shaddai to be involved in overriding natural laws. He wanted it to be a job for El Shaddai.

Once El Shaddai got involved, Sarah conceived and Isaac was born. It was a miracle. In fact, she went around town saying, "Who would ever believe an old woman like me and an old man like him could bring forth a child?" But it happened. El Shaddai got the job done. Let me make this point. El Shaddai never goes around overriding, reversing, prolonging or accelerating natural laws because He has nothing else to do. The only time He will override, reverse, prolong or accelerate a natural law is when that's what it takes to fulfill His Word.

One of the greatest examples of El Shaddai showing up is found in the book of Joshua. The warrior Joshua was faced with a battle where, in order for him to win, the sun must not set. In Genesis 1, Elohim created the sun and the moon and gave them commands: "Sun, you light the earth by day. Moon, you light the earth by night." They're both under the direction of Elohim.

In this particular situation, Joshua needed more time. The sun could not go down if he was to be victorious. (Looks like a job for El Shaddai!) Joshua pointed to the sun and the moon and commanded them to be still. "So the sun and moon stood still until the Israelites had defeated their enemies" (Josh. 10:13, *NLT*). El Shaddai overrode natural law in order that His servant could be victorious.

Jesus Himself experienced the work of El Shaddai. Everywhere He went, He manifested El Shaddai. Do you remember when Jesus first entered into public ministry? His first miracle was turning water into wine. He and His disciples were at a banquet for quite some time when the wine ran out. Jesus told them to take a pot, fill it with water (which he would supernaturally turn to wine) and offer it to the host of this party. Clearly that violated natural laws. But El Shaddai accelerated natural law. I've been told that wine takes about three years to make from the time you plant the seed that produces the vine that produces the grape and becomes the wine. El Shaddai made it happen immediately.

But the story gets better. When the official tasted the wine, he said, "Usually a host serves the best wine first . . . then, when everyone is full and doesn't care, he brings out the less expensive wines. But you have kept the best until now!" (John 2:10, *NLT*). Average-tasting wine takes about three years to make; but the best wine is a minimum six-year process. So El Shaddai didn't just accelerate something that normally takes three years. He did something that normally takes six years to do in less time than it takes to blink your eye.

What Do You Say in the Face of the Impossible?

In 1973, the Full Gospel businessmen held a world convention in Honolulu, Hawaii. I was still working for brother Copeland at that time and, normally, everywhere he went to preach, I went with him. But since he was a guest speaker at the meeting, he said there wouldn't be any need for me to go with him.

I had some vacation time on my hands, so I asked brother Copeland if Carolyn and I could go on the trip if we paid our own way. He said, "Sure." My wife and I believed God for the money, and we went. Many of the people who attended were very affluent. The men wore nice suits and their wives were decked out with diamonds. I didn't know you could wear that much jewelry! Carolyn and I felt like a couple of Gomer Pyles. We'd never seen anything like it.

At the time, the hippie movement was still going on. So there were folks who came right off the beach and into that meeting to get saved. They didn't come dressed up like the Full Gospel businessmen and their wives. They came in looking like beach bums. There was one surfer-hippie guy who showed up out of nowhere. He had the typical long hair and casual attitude. The most intelligent thing he'd ever said in his life was, "Far out!" So he came into that meeting, got saved and was filled with the Holy Spirit.

The meeting was held at the beautiful Sheraton Waikiki Hotel. It had a glass elevator that hung on the outside of the building where you could ride up to the top and catch a magnificent view of the city of Honolulu. It was quite an architectural feat in those days. I thought that was the neatest thing I'd ever seen in my life. My wife and I weren't staying in that hotel. It cost way too much money. But I told my wife that I was going to ride that elevator before I left. I'll never forget that ride as long as I live.

One night, affluent Full Gospel folk were eating at a restaurant that was at the top of the hotel. I was there when they got in the elevator to go back down to the ground level. Suddenly, the surfer bum who had just gotten saved opened the door and got in with us.

He stood there with his long hair and flip-flops, his tank top and swimming trunks and looked unbelievably out of place with the folks decked out in diamonds, expensive suits and alligator shoes. As we were going down, the elevator stopped. It just hung between floors at the top of that hotel.

Pandemonium broke out. A few moments before, all these Holy Ghost people were speaking in tongues, but now they were fearful. The beach bum, who'd only been saved a short time, looked around at the fear and panic and slowly moved to the front of the elevator. He stood right in front of all the screaming people, got down into a surfing stance and said, "Looks like a job for the Holy Ghost!" Then he prayed in tongues for a little bit, then pushed one of the elevator buttons. Immediately the elevator started moving down. Since that day, every time I hear the word "impossible," I just get into a surfer's stance and say, "Looks like a job for El Shaddai!"

Sometimes in the middle of the night, the devil will wake you up and say, "There is no way that amount of money is ever going to come into your hands." "There is no way you can be healed." "There is no way you will have what you are believing for." What do you do? You need to break out into your stance and say, "Looks like a job for El Shaddai!" The next time you go to church and someone tells you, "Dear God, we're facing the most impossible thing we've ever faced in our life," you just tell them, "Looks like a job for El Shaddai!" The next time you are at your job and someone cries, "Oh, my God, such and such happened. What are we going to do?" you just shout, "Looks like a job for El Shaddai!"

7

WAITING, FALLING, ARISING

Wait on the God of Your Salvation

The book of Micah gives us a comforting and challenging message: "Therefore I will look to the LORD; I will *wait* for the God of my salvation: my God will hear me" (Mic. 7:7, *KJV*, emphasis added). Isn't it wonderful when answers to prayers come instantly? The truth is, they usually don't. Not everything has happened instantly in my walk of faith. I've had some miracles that have happened almost as quickly as I could speak God's Word out of my mouth. I've had some manifestations that have happened within an hour of the prayer being prayed. But with the majority of my adventures in faith, I've had to wait. And wait. And wait some more.

I like to say it this way: I live between "amen" and "there it is." The moment I pray, I believe I receive. Then I start my walk of faith; I am going from "amen" to "there it is." Many times the period between the two is long. But I still have to wait. How long do most of us have to wait? That's an easy answer—until it happens. I've waited for weeks, months and even years. I've even had some things that have happened recently that took 10 years before they manifested.

I like what brother Kenneth Hagin used to say: "If you prepare to stand forever, then it won't take very long." You see, most Christians are not prepared to stand forever. They are prepared to stand for a little while. They are prepared to stand until it hurts. They are prepared to stand until more adversity comes. They are prepared to stand until persecution comes. They are prepared to stand until everybody in town says it won't work. You have got to come to the place in your life where you are prepared to stand forever, and your attitude is—"I will wait." If you have this attitude, then God will come through.

God is faithful! I seldom know how God is going to bring it about. I don't know how He is going to do it. However, I learned many years ago to stop trying to figure out how God is going to do whatever He is going to do. That's not my business. My responsibility is to believe and wait. We really have the easy part. I'm glad that I am not the one who has to remove a cancer. I just have to wait. I'm glad that I am not the one who has to gather up all the money I need. I just have to wait. I'm glad that I am not the one who has to change circumstances, alter natural laws or manipulate things to make something happen. I just have to wait. I want to challenge you to dare to stand in faith and wait.

**Stop trying to figure out how God is going
to do whatever He is going to do. That's not your business.
Your responsibility is to believe and wait.
Dare to stand in faith and wait.**

This reminds me of what happened to me a number of years ago when I left brother Kenneth Copeland's organization and launched out into my own ministry. I was traveling all over the country preaching, and I was driving everywhere. I was going to and from places like New York, L.A. and Miami. One day the Lord spoke to me and said, "I want you to start believing Me for an airplane for your ministry." I told Him, "God, I don't need an airplane. I don't even know how to fly one." "No," He said, "You don't understand. I know you don't need an airplane now, but you will need one eventually. Don't wait until the pressure is on to start believing Me for it. Do it now."

So I started believing. Now, I didn't go around telling anybody about it. I didn't send out letters about it. I didn't start preaching about it. I just believed and went about my business. Several months later, there was a greater demand on my ministry. There was no way I could do all the traveling by car. The airplane idea started making sense. It wasn't something I wanted; it was what I needed. And now I was waiting. The Lord asked me one day, "Do you believe you have received the airplane you need?" I said, "Yes!" He then asked, "So why aren't you acting like it?" *What? How are you supposed to act like you have an airplane?*

God spoke to me further, "How would it affect your schedule today if you had an airplane?" I thought for a moment and said, "I could get to more places in a shorter period of time." He told me to set up my schedule as if I had an airplane. It sounded crazy, but He was making a good point. I really needed to start acting as if I already had what I believed for. The Bible says that "faith without works is dead" (Jas. 2:26, *KJV*).

I told the man in my office who handled my scheduling to start making some phone calls. In the past, we'd had to turn down a number of invitations to preach because I couldn't get there in time by car. I told him to call all those people back and to start scheduling meetings. There was silence on the other end of the phone. I knew what he was thinking, *How on earth are we going to make this happen?* After all, he was the one who drove everywhere we preached. But he did what I asked, and when I got the schedule of where I was going, I couldn't believe it. I was set up like I already had an airplane. There was no way I could get to all these places in a car.

You would think that after I did my part, the God of my salvation would have shown up before my hectic schedule actually began. There were too many places to go and not enough time to get there by driving. So I waited on the God of my salvation. I waited for days. I waited for nights. I checked the backyard to see if my airplane was there. I checked the office and parking lot. I checked everywhere. Nothing.

The first meeting came; no airplane. I asked Him what I was to do. "Get on a commercial airline and fly there," He told me. I said, "But most of those airlines don't go to these little towns." "So fly as far as you can, and get in a car and drive the rest of the way," He replied.

Well, I did what I had to do and somehow managed to make that meeting. It wasn't easy. I had no idea how I was going to continue keeping my hectic schedule. I didn't know how He was going to give me the airplane that I desperately needed. But my job was simply to wait. A year and a half went by, and I was still waiting. At some point, our organization hired a man for a management position. Unbeknownst to anyone, he had more than 10,000 hours of flying experience. When I found that out, I thought, "There's my pilot!" Finally something was happening.

Some time later, I was invited by some folks from a little town in west Texas to preach to a handful of people. When I got there

I found out I was going to be preaching in an abandoned Laundromat. It was the only place these people could find to hold this meeting. The man who organized it told me that the local church didn't want us in there, so the only place available was this old building. I didn't think too much about it because I had preached in all kinds of places—bowling alleys, service stations; I even preached in a lounge once.

I got over to that abandoned Laundromat and there were no pews, not even any real seats to speak of. It certainly did not have the makings of a successful meeting. I preached with a broken-down dryer as my podium for about 3 days in front of 12 people.

Right in the middle of one of the services, a man came walking through the back door. He looked like he weighed at least 275 pounds. He had dust all over his bib overalls and wore a straw hat. In a real deep voice he told me, "God sent me. I was plowing my field and God told me to come here because some preacher boy needs my help. I don't go nowhere unless God tells me to." His said his name was Oop.

As he stood there telling me how God told him I needed his help, I was wondering where in the world this guy came from! He looked like the least likely to be used of God to meet my need. Then he said, "God told me that you need an airplane." That sure got my attention. You have to remember that I had never mentioned, preached or talked about this need to anyone. Oop reached into the pockets of his dusty overalls and started pulling out money. Just before he walked out the door of the building, Oop said, "God told me to give you that for that airplane, boy.

Now God has told me to leave, and I won't be back 'less God tells me." When I counted the money, it wasn't enough for an airplane, but it was a good start. The God of my salvation was showing up. What next? Wait some more.

While you are sitting and reading this book, God is out there working on your behalf in your situation. If you are willing to wait, what you are waiting for will happen. Don't give up!

I went off to Omaha, Nebraska, to preach at a convention with brother Fred Price. We had been there all week. After the meeting was over, we all headed back to the airport. My wife and I were getting ready to get on a flight to go back to Texas, and brother Fred and his wife, Betty, were headed back to their home in Los Angeles. As we parted ways to get to our gates, it hit me like a ton of bricks. I turned around and started yelling in the middle of the terminal to get brother Fred's attention.

"What do you want?" he yelled back. I shouted, "Fred, I just wanted to tell you that I am not moved by this. I believe I've got my own airplane. It's coming!" All the people in the airport looked at brother Fred and me like we were a couple of nuts. But I didn't care. It wasn't their airplane; it was mine. And it was coming.

When I got back home, our office manager picked up my wife and me. He handed me a note with the name and number of a couple that Carolyn and I were friends with. They said it was very important that I call them back that night, and they even wanted to meet with us for dinner. I called them that evening, and we made plans to have dinner at a local restaurant in Dallas. So there I was, sitting at the table minding my own business and enjoying some crabmeat when one of them said, "Brother Jerry, the reason we called you to have dinner is because God told us to give you an airplane."

Boy, I was so excited I almost threw my crabmeat in the air! They said that a year and a half previously, God had told them that the airplane they were flying belonged to me. The problem was they owed several thousand dollars on it, and God wanted it given to me debt free. So for a year and a half they waited on God to have it paid off. And there I was for a year and a half waiting on the God of my salvation for an airplane. I had no idea these people were believing God for the money to pay it off. The entire time I was waiting, God was working. I want to submit to you while you are sitting and reading this book that God is out there working on your behalf for your particular situation. If you are willing to wait, what you are waiting for will happen. Don't give up!

Don't Let the Devil Rejoice Over Your Stumbles

Read what else Micah wrote. "Rejoice not against me, O mine enemy: when I fall, I shall arise; when I sit in darkness, the LORD shall be a light unto me" (Mic. 7:8, *KJV*). Do you know what happens when you are waiting on God? The devil tries to convince you that it won't happen. He tells you that it won't come to pass. He starts putting pressure on you. He tries to tempt you to give up. He whispers negative things in your ears. He is waiting for you to quit.

When does your enemy rejoice against you? When you fall. When you make mistakes. When you slip up. When you don't resist temptation. When you yield to pressure. When you don't obey God. When you make vows one day and forget them the next. The devil loves it when you stumble. You've probably heard him ridicule you. You've heard him intimidate you. You thought you were really trying to live by faith, but you messed up and the devil started laughing.

It's time for you to stand up and shout, "Devil, you are not laughing at me anymore." How do you stop Satan's laughter? How do you stop his rejoicing? Don't yield to his pressures. Don't yield to his attacks. Don't yield to his accusations.

Get Up!

Micah said, "When I *fall*, I shall *arise*." Notice that he had fallen. He stumbled. All of us have stumbled and fallen at all times. We have all missed it. We have all blown it. We have all made mistakes. We have all come short of the glory of God. The worst thing you can do when you fall is refuse to get up. If you trip, the most natural thing to do is to get up. You wouldn't stay on the ground forever, would you? No, you would just get up. Which one do you think is the bigger and better person: the one who stumbles and lies around for the rest of his or her life, wallowing in self-pity because he/she made a mistake, or the one who stumbles, gets up, moves on, cuts the strings to his or her past and says, "Yes, I fell. Big deal! My God is bigger than my mistake. I am going on." If you fall, the cycle is not complete until you rise again.

I was preaching in Hot Springs, Arkansas, and walking across a huge platform while preaching when I fell off the back of the platform. Guess where I landed? In the bass drum. But I jumped out of that drum and kept right on preaching. I never even made a reference to my fall. I acted like that was the way I preached all the time. Sure, it was embarrassing. I felt like an idiot sitting there in the bass drum. But I would have looked worse than an idiot if I hadn't gotten out and gotten up. What on earth would those people in the audience have thought about me if they had come back the next night and I was still sitting in that bass drum?

All of us have stumbled and fallen at times.
The worst thing you can do is refuse to get up.

I remember watching a man in a shopping mall who was getting ready to go down an escalator. This was way back in the mid-seventies when things like high-heeled, platform shoes for men were all the rage. This guy was all decked out in a fancy white suit, a white felt hat with a feather in it, the funniest looking pair of sunglasses and those crazy shoes. When he stepped on the escalator, one of his heels got caught right in the middle of one of the steps. All of a sudden, this guy started falling all the way down the escalator. As he was falling, his funny sunglasses flew off his face. But when he got down to the bottom, he landed on his feet. He reached down, picked up his sunglasses, and said, "Well, all right then," and walked off. He acted like that was how he rode the escalator all the time. Every time the devil tries to trip me up and make me fall, I think about that man on the escalator. I tell Satan, "Well, all right then," and I move on.

There comes a time and a place in your life when you finally have to decide once and for all that if you fall down it doesn't mean the end of the world. Many people have come up to me and said, "But, brother Jerry, you don't know how far I have fallen." It makes no difference. You can't get so far down that God won't pick you up. "The steps of the godly are directed by the LORD. He delights in every detail of their lives. Though they stumble, they will never fall, for the LORD holds them by the hand" (Ps. 37:23-24, *NLT*). If you fall, know that God is not finished with you. He doesn't think you are of no use to Him. He says, "Look up. I'm holding your hand."

If you are willing to be picked up, God will pick you up. If you will to get up, nothing can keep you down. Your neighbor can't keep you down. Your coworkers can't keep you down. You belong standing up. Your finances can't keep you down. Your tired body can't keep you down. You don't belong down. God will go to any length to get you up. If He has to admonish you, encourage you or stand in your face and rebuke you, He will do it until you get up. I want you to get it into your spirit that if you fall, it's not over until you get up again. Don't ever look at your fall and magnify it. Keep your eyes on getting up.

When a child is born, it knows nothing about walking. It's never even had a thought about walking. There's never been a baby born who, the minute it came out of the womb and the doctor spanked its behind, said, "Thanks, I needed that," and walked away. Babies are helpless. They just lie around and are totally dependent on somebody else for everything. Sooner or later, though, they start finding out some things. They start learning how to communicate and realize that when they cry, someone comes.

The first time I ever saw my oldest daughter, Jerriann, was when she was three-and-a-half months old. I was stationed at Fort Dix when she was born, so I didn't get to be there at her birth. I remember one day watching her in the crib, and all of a sudden she started moving her legs around. I said to Carolyn, "What's the matter with our kid?" She laughed and said, "Nothing. She's finding out that she has legs. She's exercising her muscles." Jerriann kept lying in that crib, but every once in a while, she discovered something new about her body. She started watching and moving her fingers. She started watching and moving her hands. She started watching and moving her toes.

When she was about seven months old, she was already sitting up and crawling and wanting to walk. She was probably thinking, "Everyone else is walking. Why can't I?" One day our family was sitting on the living room floor. I was at one end of the room and Carolyn was at the other. My wife was holding our daughter up by the waist. She had never taken a step before on her own. I told my little girl, "Come to Daddy, Jerriann. Come to Daddy." She looked at me with this huge ol' grin across her face. She wanted to come to me real bad, but something wouldn't work. I finally told Carolyn to let go of Jerriann so she could try to walk on her own.

When babies take those first steps, and they fall, they don't lie there and stop trying. They don't give up and say, "I just can't do it. I can't walk." They instinctively know that when they fall, they will rise. They get up and try another step. It doesn't look much like walking, of course, but it's a start. After much effort and many spills, my daughter eventually made it into her daddy's arms.

When we are born again, we are not born a spiritual adult. We are born a spiritual baby. Like newborn babies, "you must crave pure spiritual milk so that you can grow into the fullness of your salvation. Cry out for this nourishment" (1 Pet. 2:2, *NLT*). We've never been in this spiritual place before in our lives. We don't know anything about walking by faith. But God is telling us, "Come to Daddy." And there we are, taking our first steps and falling flat on our faces. But we can't quit. We can't give up. We can't stay down. If we keep at it, we will make it to Daddy.

8

THROW IN THE TOWEL OR STICK IT OUT

Don't Quit

Success is about striving to obtain everything that God has promised is yours, no matter how long it takes and no matter what kind of obstacles you might face. Success does not mean you never have problems; it means you know how to overcome them. There is no such thing as a life on this planet without problems. We are always going to be confronted with adversity, trials and tests of all kinds. It's our attitude about these problems that will determine whether we fail or succeed.

"Do not throw away this confident trust in the Lord, no matter what happens. Remember the great reward it brings you! Patient endurance is what you need now, so you will continue to do God's will. Then you will receive all that he has promised" (Heb. 10:35-36, *NLT*). There is a reward promised to those who will not give up. There is a reward promised to those who will stick to it. I don't see anywhere in the Bible where people who quit are rewarded. It's only those who develop staying power. *THE MESSAGE* says it like this, "So don't throw it all away now. You were sure of yourselves then. It's still a sure thing! But you need to stick it out, staying with God's plan so you'll be there for the promised completion." You have come too far to quit. You need to stick it out. You are not a quitter; you are a winner!

Staying Power

The book of James gives us something important to think about. "Take, my brethren, the prophets, who have spoken in the name of the Lord, for an example of suffering affliction, and of patience.

Behold, we count them happy which endure. Ye have heard of the patience of Job, and have seen *the end of the Lord;* that the Lord is very pitiful, and of tender mercy" (Jas. 5:10-11, *KJV,* emphasis added). *THE MESSAGE* puts it this way: "Take the old prophets as your mentors. They put up with anything, went through every-thing, and never once quit, all the time honoring God. What a gift life is to those who stay the course! You've heard, of course, of Job's staying power, and you know how God brought it all together for him at the end. That's because God cares, cares right down to the last detail."

When I read these verses, one sentence kept rising up in my spirit: "You've heard, of course, of Job's staying power, and you know how God brought it all together for him at the end." In fact, I was scheduled to preach in a church in Pasadena, Texas, on a par-ticular Wednesday night. I was sitting on the front row during the praise and worship, and as I was getting ready to go to the pulpit to preach, the Spirit of God told me I was to preach on this topic that night. I kept hearing the phrase, "I am going to bring it all together for you" over and over. I could hardly wait to preach and hear what the Holy Spirit had to say about these verses.

There are several points these Scriptures reveal to us that will help us experience victory when we are going through difficult situations.

1. No matter what you might go through, don't quit.
2. No matter how impossible your situation may seem, stay on course.

3. When your problems seem more than you can bear, develop staying power.

4. When it seems that nothing is happening, remember that God is about to bring it all together for you.

It appears to me that one of the greatest needs in the Body of Christ today is "staying power." There are way too many believers who give up too quickly. They're ready to throw in the towel at the first sign of adversity. These verses in James talk about Job, with whom most of us are familiar. Man, talk about somebody who experienced adversity. And I'm talking every day for a period of between 9 and 12 months.

One of the greatest needs in the Body of Christ today is "staying power." Too many believers are giving up too quickly.

It's important that you understand that the book of Job does not cover this man's lifetime. Most theologians agree that it only covers around a year of his life. This book tells me that when the devil pulls out the heavy artillery and fires it at a man for 12 solid months, day in and day out, God can still turn the situation around. If you are going through the worst time in your life right now, it's not over yet. It's not over until you see "the end of the Lord." That phrase doesn't mean that God will no longer exist or cease to be. It means it's not over until God has had His say in the matter.

You have got to wait for the end of the Lord. It's not over until God has done His part. God is working behind the scenes even as you read this book. And when you have seen the end of the Lord, that means God has brought it all together for you.

What was the end of the Lord regarding Job? "And the LORD turned the captivity of Job, when he prayed for his friends: also the LORD gave Job twice as much as he had before . . . the LORD blessed the latter end of Job more than his beginning" (Job 42:10,12, *KJV*). That's what James was referring to.

Have you experienced your turnaround yet? If not, then it's not over yet. You have not seen the end of the Lord. Have you experienced restoration yet? If not, then it's not over yet. You have not seen the end of the Lord. Are you better off now than you were before this attack came? If not, then it's not over yet. You have not seen the end of the Lord. If you are determined that you are going to stick it out, you are going to see the end of the Lord.

Stick It Out!

The *King James Version* calls staying power, patience. Being patient means to be constant or consistent. It means never changing, regardless of the circumstances. Not enough people today are willing to be patient for a very long time. They give up at the drop of a hat. They're not consistent. Robert Schuller is famous for saying, "Tough times never last, but tough people do." Success as well as failure is a choice. Success begins when you decide you aren't going to quit. Failure begins when you decide you can't take it anymore.

I realize that all of us from time to time are confronted with impossible situations, and we can get to a point where we think we just can't take it anymore. But the reality is that we don't know how much we can take until we push ourselves. By now you know I'm a boxing fanatic. It never ceases to amaze me that if these athletes are in good condition and if they have trained properly, though it might seem in a moment during a fight that they are finished, they can suddenly get a second wind and completely turn the tide.

I remember Evander Holyfield's three most famous fights with Riddick Bowe. Talk about staying power. There were times when it looked like there was absolutely no way that Evander could win. Yet he never gave up. He wouldn't quit. Finally, that second wind came. I will never forget watching one particular fight and hearing the announcer say, "It looks like Evander has finally come to the end of the line." When the second wind hit and he won the fight, that same announcer said, "We have just seen a legend at work."

You don't know how much you can take until you are willing to push yourself. I promise you, you can take a whole lot more than you think you can. Remember that you are filled with the Greater One. "Greater is he that is in you, than he that is in the world" (1 John 4:4, *KJV*). I am not talking about our own strength, our own might or our own ability. The Greater One indwells us. I have reached points in my life when it felt like I couldn't take anymore. But I wouldn't say it, because to say it would admit that the blood of Jesus wasn't enough. To say it would be to say the Cross didn't work; but it did work. If I can't take what the devil dishes out, then Jesus died in vain. And we all know that's not true.

Notice that both James and the writer of the book of Hebrews agree that we have to stick it out if we expect to be victorious and if we want to be rewarded. Hebrews admonishes us to "be not slothful, but followers of them who through faith and patience inherit the promises" (Heb. 6:12, *KJV*), or in *THE MESSAGE*, "Be like those who stay the course with committed faith and then get everything promised to them." Don't get lazy where your faith is concerned. You can only stay on course when you have committed faith.

It's Not Over Until God Says It's Over

I like to say; "Don't ever rule God out." Let Him have the last say. Your situation may look so impossible at this moment that you have decided to accept the worst. King David did that one time. "Tell me, what's going on, GOD? How long do I have to live? Give me the bad news!" (Ps. 39:4, *THE MESSAGE*). David was saying, "Give it to me. Just give me the worst." This is what a lot of people do. They accept defeat as final when defeat is not inevitable. Don't say, "Okay, I will just learn to live with this. I guess this is my lot in life. That stuff may work for some, but not for all of us. I guess I'm one of the ones it doesn't work for." It is going to work for you if you develop staying power; if you hold on to the Word of God; if you don't cast away your confidence.

We don't know how God is going to bring it all together for us. In fact, most of the time, we don't have a clue. Be honest. When God has given you a breakthrough, did you know in advance how He was going to do it? Of course not. We just have to let God be God. He is smarter than us anyway. And He's got a number of ways that He can meet your need without you trying to figure it out on your own.

"Endings are better than beginnings. Sticking to it is better than standing out" (Eccles. 7:8, *THE MESSAGE*). Believe that your situation is going to get better. Believe that it's going to turn out better than you can ask or think. You have to ask yourself where your staying power is. Have you let go of it or are you holding fast? We have to stay focused on the end of the Lord. This is what we are waiting for.

"Mark the perfect man, and behold the upright: for the end of that man is *peace*" (Ps. 37:37, *KJV,* emphasis added). Peace can be translated as wellbeing, soundness and wholeness. It can also be defined as prosperity. The *Amplified Bible* says, "There is a happy end for the man of peace." The *NIV* says, "There is a future for the man of peace." Sounds to me that if this man determines that he is not going to give up, if he is going to stick with it, if he is going to trust God all the way, then he is going to have a happy ending. And it is going to bring peace, wellbeing, soundness, wholeness and prosperity.

"He [God] is their strength in the time of trouble. And the LORD shall help them, and deliver them: he shall deliver them from the wicked, and save them, because they trust in him" (Ps. 37:39-40, *KJV*). The book of Deuteronomy offers that if we keep walking in God's ways, God will "do thee good at thy latter end" (Deut. 8:16, *KJV*).

God is going to do some good things. It's not over yet. You need to tell the devil that he hasn't seen the end of you yet. You need to tell him that your best days are ahead of you. If the devil keeps bringing up your future, bring up his. His is not very bright, but yours is. You are headed for some great things. You are headed for a turnaround. You are headed for restoration. You are headed for the double. And where is Satan headed? To the Lake of Fire. If you remind him of that, it'll shut him up pretty quick.

Someone once said, "There is nothing that perseverance cannot accomplish." Someone else said, "If I persist long enough, then I know I will win." It's your choice. You can either give up now or you can stick with it and watch God bring it all together for you.

Let's look at a couple more verses in both the *King James Version* and *THE MESSAGE* translations:

"Therefore seeing we have this ministry, as we have received mercy, we faint not" (2 Cor. 4:1, *KJV*). "We're not about to throw up our hands and walk off the job just because we run into occasional hard times" (*THE MESSAGE*).

"We are troubled on every side, yet not distressed" (2 Cor. 4:8, *KJV*). "We've been surrounded and battered by troubles, but we're not demoralized" (*THE MESSAGE*).

"For our light affliction, which is but for a moment, worketh for us a far more exceeding and eternal weight of glory" (2 Cor. 4:17, *KJV*). "These hard times are small potatoes compared to the coming good times" (*THE MESSAGE*).

"While we look not at the things which are seen, but at the things which are not seen: for the things which are seen are temporal; but the things which are not seen are eternal" (2 Cor. 4:18, *KJV*). "There's far more here than meets the eye" (*THE MESSAGE*).

"For we walk by faith, not by sight" (2 Cor. 5:7, *KJV*). "It's what we trust in but don't yet see that keeps us going" (*THE MESSAGE*).

We need to develop our staying power. We need to get tough. We need to get some backbone. We need to learn how to set our jaw. We need to learn how to put our hand to the plow and not look back. We need to make up our minds that if anybody is going to give up, it's going to be the devil, not us. You need to fully expect to see the end of the Lord. You need to fully believe that God is going to bring it together for you. Make up your mind that this is your time for restoration. This is your time for double. This is your time for harvest. This is your time for reaping. This is your time to be totally free.

Don't Give Up . . . Good Things Are Coming Your Way

I was reading Psalm 126 one day and the Lord brought to my attention some things I'd like to share with you. This is the psalm:

When the LORD turned again the captivity of Zion, we were like them that dream. Then was our mouth filled with laughter, and our tongue with singing: then said they among the heathen, The LORD hath done great things for them. The LORD hath done great things for us; whereof we are glad. Turn again our captivity, O LORD, as the streams in the south. They that sow in tears shall reap in joy. He that goeth forth and weepeth, bearing precious seed, shall doubtless come again with rejoicing, bringing his sheaves with him.

I was struck by the phrase "The Lord hath done great things." I want you to meditate on that and really allow it to sink deep down into your spirit. God is about to do some great things. He has done great things in times past, but He is about to do some more great things—perhaps even greater things than you might even imagine. You may be reading this book desperate for a breakthrough. You might be on the verge of throwing in the towel. You may need a turnaround like you have never needed it before. But this is not the time to give up. If you can hang on a little longer, you are going to find out that some good things are coming your way.

THE MESSAGE translates the ending of this psalm this way: "So those who went off with heavy hearts will come home laughing, with armloads of blessing." Could you use some laughter right now? Could you use an armload of blessings? The difference in whether or not you experience that something good—that laughter and that armload of blessing—is determined by whether what you are believing for is a desire or just a wish. There's a big difference between the two.

Jesus said, "Therefore I say unto you, What things soever ye desire, when ye pray, believe that ye receive them, and ye shall have them" (Mark 11:24, *KJV*). As I was listening to the Spirit of God regarding this, He said, "Without genuine desire, your faith will be lifeless." I don't want lifeless faith. Faith comes alive when there is desire—a genuine and intense desire—and not just a wish for something to happen.

Nearly everything I have ever desired with great intensity has come to pass in my life. If I wanted it badly enough, and if I pressed toward getting it, it came to pass. Desire dictates how much you really want something. Desire is what causes you to stay focused. Desire is what keeps you going when others have given up. Desire is what enables you to stand when others have quit. Desire is what keeps you enthusiastic.

Someone once said, "Nothing great has ever been achieved without enthusiasm." Enthusiasm is a must if you expect to see God's promises become realities. While you are between "amen" and "there it is," you can lose your joy. People who lose their joy aren't likely to become winners. You've got to be enthusiastic about what you are believing God for.

What Do You See?

If you really want your breakthrough, you had better get a vision for it and refuse to let it go. Vision is the ability to see things not seen by the natural eye. Second Corinthians 4:18 says, "We look not at the things which are seen, but at the things which are not seen" (*KJV*). Through the eyes of faith, I see some good things coming my way. Through the eyes of faith, I see that breakthrough. Through the eyes of faith, I can see that financial need being met.

Through the eyes of faith, I can see that turnaround I am believing God for.

You can only receive what you can see yourself receiving. Close your eyes right now and visualize what you want, and say, "I can see some good things coming my way." Imagine your bills paid in full. Imagine the miracle you need for your family coming to pass. Imagine that healing you need for your body. This is how you get your breakthrough.

It's easy for most people to see bad things coming their way. Why is it so hard for us to see good things? It is the way we have been programmed. We have to reprogram our minds to see good coming into our lives. We need to stretch our imagination. Albert Einstein once said, "Your imagination is your preview of life's coming attractions." If you go to watch a movie in a theater, you also see previews of about three other movies before the one you came to see. Your imagination is the preview of your life's coming attractions. Your imagination is a gift from God. Without your imagination you can't picture God's promises coming to pass in your life. You have to let it work for you, not against you.

In the book of Hebrews, we see a man's imagination working for him in a positive way. "By faith he [Moses] forsook Egypt, not fearing the wrath of the king: for he endured, as seeing him who is invisible" (Heb. 11:27, *KJV*). Moses was able to endure the circumstances he was confronted with. Why? Because he saw something that could not be seen with the natural eye. *THE MESSAGE* says that Moses "was looking ahead, anticipating the payoff" (v. 26). I love that. The word "recompense" is the *King James* word for "payday." Moses imagined a payday, so to speak. "Cast not away therefore your confidence, which hath great recompense of reward" (Heb. 10:35, *KJV*). Payday comes to those who refuse to give up.

This is what kept Moses going when his mind screamed at him, *What's the use? You are wasting your time. Nothing is happening. Why do you keep doing this faith thing?* And this is what will keep you going too. You need to anticipate your payday. You need to anticipate an armload of blessings. You need to anticipate your time of laughter and rejoicing.

"We can make a large horse turn around and go wherever we want by means of a small bit in its mouth. And a tiny rudder makes a huge ship turn wherever the pilot wants it to go, even though the winds are strong" (Jas. 3:3-4, *NLT*). You can cause a horse to have a turnaround by putting a bit in his mouth. You can cause a great ship to have a turnaround by controlling the rudder.

"In the same way, the tongue is a small thing that makes grand speeches. But a tiny spark can set a great forest on fire. And the tongue is a flame of fire. It is a whole world of wickedness, corrupting your entire body. It can set your whole life on fire, for it is set on fire by hell itself" (Jas. 3:5-6, *NLT*). Your tongue acts like a bit or a rudder. You can turn your circumstances around by speaking right words. Stop saying, "Nothing good ever happens to me," and start saying, "Some good things are coming my way."

Psychologists have estimated that we can hear up to 500 words a minute in our mind. For most people, 498 of those words are negative. Here is an important biblical principle. What you hear repeatedly forms what you believe. "Faith cometh by hearing, and hearing the word of God" (Rom. 10:17, *KJV*). If you have these 500 words crossing your mind every minute and most of them are negative thoughts, the more you hear them the more you are going to believe them. You believe what is going on inside your mind. When what you believe drops down into your spirit, then your spirit is designed by God to make those thoughts and beliefs come to pass.

Jesus said it this way, "The good man brings good things out of the good stored up in him, and the evil man brings evil things out of the evil stored up in him" (Matt. 12:35, *NIV*). If you believe that you will fail, then what you believe and speak will come to pass. If you believe that you will have a breakthrough, then what you believe and speak will come to pass. It's your choice what you will believe. It's your choice what you will speak.

It doesn't take any more energy to be positive than it does to be negative. We don't have to psych ourselves out. It's like driving a car. It doesn't take more effort to put it in reverse than it does to put it in drive. You don't have to sit there and pray, "Oh God, give me the energy to put this thing in reverse." No, you just shift the gears and it's done. It is all about what you choose to do.

"Don't be afraid, my people! Be glad now and rejoice because the LORD has done great things" (Joel 2:21, *NLT*). If you truly believe that God is about to cause some good things to come your way, then you have to act as though it is already happening. Act on what Joel wrote. Notice he didn't say, "When good things come, be glad and rejoice." He said, "Be glad and rejoice" first. Often we want to wait until we can see the manifestation before we rejoice and be glad. But that's backwards in the mind of God.

You need to get rid of fear, and start being glad and start re-joicing, even if in the natural it doesn't appear that there is any-thing to rejoice about. This is where staying power kicks in. This is where desire kicks in. This is where faith kicks. We do it even if we don't feel like it. We do it even if in our mind it looks fool-ish. We do it even if others think we're crazy. Show the devil through your rejoicing and being glad that you no longer believe his lies. Show him that there is no way that he is going to keep you down. Show him that you believe what God says more than what he says.

"Worship GOD if you want the best; worship opens doors to all his goodness" (Ps. 34:9, *THE MESSAGE*).

"O my soul, bless GOD. From head to toe, I'll bless his holy name! O my soul, bless GOD, don't forget a single bless-ing! . . . God makes everything come out right" (Ps. 103:1-2,6, *THE MESSAGE*).

"Thank GOD because He's good. . . . The hand of GOD has turned the tide! The hand of GOD is raised in victory! The hand of GOD has turned the tide!" (Ps. 118:1,15-16, *THE MESSAGE*).

"Hallelujah! It's a good thing to sing praise to our God. . . . GOD puts the fallen on their feet again" (Ps. 147:1,6, *THE MESSAGE*).

There is a story in the Old Testament about something the prophet Elijah told the people of God to do in preparation for a coming event. This prophet told them to dig ditches in order to catch the water from the rain that was coming. But there was a problem. There was a serious drought in the land. The people had not seen rain in a long time. There had not even been a cloud in the sky. Yet the Word of God came to them to dig a ditch. "Rain is coming," God said. "You'd better get ready for it."

If most of us had been there, we would have said something like, "I am not digging a ditch until I at least see a cloud." God doesn't work that way. He wanted them to dig while there was no evidence in the natural that rain was coming. These people were told to act as though the results they desired were going to happen. So what happened? After the ditches were dug, the rain came.

I'm quite sure at some point that the people out there digging ditches looked up to see if any clouds had come. They were probably getting frustrated and disappointed as they were digging. They were probably on the verge of throwing in the towel. But the prophet Elijah kept telling them, "Just keeping digging. Don't give up. Don't quit. Don't throw in the towel. Keep digging. The rain is coming."

We need to dig a little more. And we need to dance, sing and shout while digging. We need to remember it's not over until God says it's over. We need to hang in there and stop whining. We need to keep on digging until we see our breakthrough. I promise you that if you continue to do those things, your manifestation will come. If you don't give up and if you don't quit; if you don't throw in the towel, you will receive what you are believing for (see 2 Kings 3:16-17).

9

THE FOURTH MAN

Don't Compromise

In the third chapter of Daniel, we have the record of three Hebrew children who dared to believe God. Let me give you a bit of history about this story. King Nebuchadnezzar had taken captive some of Israel's young, mighty men. He then established a decree that whenever a specific sound of special musical instruments rang out, the people were to fall down and worship the golden statue that King Nebuchadnezzar had erected of himself. Whoever refused to bow down would be thrown into a furnace of fire. These instruments rang out one day, and three Hebrew men—Shadrach, Meshach and Abednego—did not bow down and worship this idol. One of the things I want to share with you is something Dr. Oral Roberts taught me years ago: He said, "If you don't bow, then you won't burn."

The law of compromise is if you bow, then you burn. I remember something brother Kenneth Copeland said to me as we were driving to a meeting one time. He pointed his finger at me and said, "Jerry, anything you compromise to get, you will ultimately lose." At the time, I didn't understand that fully. But as I began to learn more about the principles of faith and what it meant to stand on God's Word, I figured it out. Once you receive a revelation from God, then you need to decide that you are going to live by it no matter what. If you start to compromise, however, then you will eventually fail.

The devil loves to cause people to compromise. The devil loves to put pressure on us until we back off. The devil loves to get you in a situation where while you are standing for healing, he creates enough symptoms in your body so that you start believing that healing is impossible. Compromise is a major problem in the Church today. However, when you get a revelation of who you are in Christ and what belongs to you, then compromise is out of the question. Why compromise if God is on your side? Why compromise if you know how it's going to turn out?

The Bible tells me that God is going to deliver me from all my adversities. Why wouldn't He? I'm His child. I'm the righteousness of God. I'm a son of God just like Jesus is. Why wouldn't God deliver me? Jesus said, "Father, show them that you love them as much as you love me." If I can see God delivering Jesus out of trouble, then I can expect Him to deliver Jerry out of it too. And since I know this is true, then there is no need to compromise.

Let's say that somebody told me, "Brother Jerry, the Lord has dealt with me about giving you one million dollars. At the end of the month, I'm going to send you that money." In the meantime, there could be an attack in my finances, and it could look as though everything is falling apart. I might not have a dime, and it might appear that there is no way I'll overcome it. If this man who promised me the money is a man of his word, then I know he'll be faithful and won't compromise. Therefore, I know how the situation is going to turn out.

Why compromise when the heat is on? Why compromise because of the present circumstances? The Bible says, "Many are the afflictions of the righteous: but the LORD delivereth him out of them all" (Ps. 34:19, *KJV*). See, if you refuse to compromise, then you *will* be delivered from your situation. Most of the time when the *Amplified Bible* uses the word "righteous," it is prefixed with the word "uncompromisingly." We need to become the uncompromisingly righteous.

Turn the Pressure Around

King Nebuchadnezzar commanded the inhabitants of the land to bow or burn. But these three Hebrew men refused to compromise. Here is what happened.

> Then Nebuchadnezzar flew into a rage and ordered Shadrach, Meshach, and Abednego to be brought before him. When they were brought in, Nebuchadnezzar said to them, "Is it true, Shadrach, Meshach, and Abednego, that you refuse to serve my gods or to worship the gold statue I have set up? I will give you one more chance. If you bow down and worship the statue I have made when you hear the sound of the musical instruments, all will be well. But if you refuse, you will be thrown immediately into the blazing furnace. What god will be able to rescue you from my power then?" (Dan. 3:13-15, *NLT*).

This is a perfect example of the way the devil challenges the children of God today. The devil doesn't play fair. What he loves to do is create enough pressure to get you to back off. Don't think that I've never been challenged. We all are challenged at one time or another. Many times I have been tempted to give up, but I've had to cast down those thoughts.

Satan is a compromiser. He doesn't want you to know this. The same God who said, "Let there be light" and there was light, also proclaimed, "Resist the devil and he will flee from you." The same powerful word of God that created the universe has already been spoken over the devil. So Satan has to compromise or break down when pressure is applied, and the pressure that you must apply is through speaking the Word of God.

The same God who said, "Let there be light" and there was light, also proclaimed, "Resist the devil and he will flee from you." Satan has to compromise or break down when pressure is applied, and the pressure that you must apply is through speaking the Word of God.

The Bible tells us that God "turned" the captivity of Job. As I spent time studying this phrase, I began to realize that what this means in common vernacular is "to turn the tables." It's one thing to get someone free from some pressure situation, but it's something else to then put that pressure back on the enemy.

Pressure is not fun. It's not comfortable. I've had times when I got up in the middle of the night, walked out to my backyard and screamed at the devil. I found out that God would not allow the devil to put anything on me that I was not able to bear. He would always provide a way of escape for me. God started turning my captivity around. I kept confessing the Word over and over and over again until the devil couldn't take it anymore, and he fled. It's time for you to put some pressure on the devil.

The Power We Have in Jesus

King Nebuchadnezzar was one of the proudest men that ever lived. He thought of himself as a god. He had built a city that was second to none. He had constructed a fortress that was magnificent. The architecture of his city was the finest of any city that had ever been built. There had never been any man as mighty and more oppressive to the children of Israel than this king.

Satan has even more pride. He especially loves being praised. When Jesus was hanging on the cross, and He cried out, "My God, My God, why hast thou forsaken me?" Satan was convinced he had won, and all of his domain began to rejoice. They thought Jesus had failed in His mission to redeem mankind. Satan was receiving the cheers and congratulations from all his cohorts. In his mind he was being exalted even above God, because he thought that he had defeated Jesus and that he had defeated God. And as far as his cohorts were concerned, Satan was champion.

For three-and-a-half years during His public ministry, Jesus dealt Satan nothing but misery. Satan and his cohorts couldn't touch Him. Satan couldn't make people sick fast enough because Jesus healed them one after another. He couldn't cause people to be filled with demons fast enough because Jesus cast them out one after another. He couldn't keep people blind because Jesus opened their eyes. He couldn't keep people deaf because Jesus would unstop their ears. He couldn't keep people in bondage because Jesus would set them free. You can imagine how frustrated Satan must have been.

But then one day Jesus dropped His guard and allowed Satan to take Him captive. He hung on the cross dying, and questioned why God had forsaken Him. And Satan's domain began to celebrate. They didn't totally understand it, of course. They didn't know why during those three-and-a-half years they couldn't touch him. They tried their best. They tried to push Him off a cliff. They tried to stone Him. They tried to trip Him up by the religious leaders. Nothing worked. Jesus was in control of every situation during that entire time.

When Jesus was taken by the soldiers, bound and shackled, to Pilate's court, they saw a side of Jesus they had never seen before. He was bound. He was stripped of His clothes. He was blindfolded. He was slugged. He was spit upon. He was bruised and battered. And as far as they were concerned, Satan had finally gotten to Jesus. They began to incite the people into crucifying Jesus. The crowd went wild. They began yelling, "Crucify Him. Crucify Him. Crucify Him." And He was crucified. When Jesus took His last breath, the party in Satan's domain began. Satan was worshiped as their champion. He was lifted up in pride.

**God had turned the universe over to Jesus;
and now Jesus is saying to you and me that we
don't have to be a slave to Satan any longer.
We now have authority.**

But on the third day after Jesus' death, as they were rejoicing and telling Satan what a master he was, something happened. The Bible says that Jesus was justified. His blood had paid the price. God said, "It's enough. Let My Son go." And Jesus walked right over to Satan, and the first thing He did was strip the devil of the armor he trusted in. Then he took back the keys of death, hell and the grave. Hell itself was left in shambles. The rejoicing ceased. Jesus left Satan absolutely powerless.

Jesus ascended from the region of the damned and then He stood before the throne of God, who anointed Jesus with the oil of gladness, put the scepter of righteousness into His hands and gave Him His throne. This was Jesus' inauguration day. God turned the universe over to Jesus. But that was not the end of it. Jesus immediately descended back into Earth and He appeared to His disciples. The first thing He said to them was, "I have been given all authority in heaven and on earth" (Matt. 28:18, *NLT*). This means that all the power the devil once had now belonged to Jesus. Jesus then commanded His disciples to go and heal the sick and cast out devils in His name. God had turned the universe over to Jesus; and now Jesus is saying to you and me that we don't have to be a slave to Satan any longer.

We now have authority. And if we do, then why should we compromise? Why should we quit? Why should we give up? You might be thinking, *But, brother Jerry, you don't know how hard it is. You don't know how long I've been standing.* If you get a revelation of the power and the authority you have, then you are about to experience victory like never before.

God Is Able and Will Deliver You

Paul wrote, "I know whom I have believed, and am persuaded that he is able" (2 Tim. 1:12, *KJV*). God is able. The reason a lot of people compromise is simply because they don't know that God is able to deliver them. When you are fully persuaded that He is able to deliver you, then you will never bow down again. And guess what? You won't burn either!

Once again I learned from Oral Roberts that the law of compromise is if *you bow, you burn.* If you fold up, you lose. The Lord said to me one time, "Son, I want to tell you something, and I don't want you to ever forget it. Every time there is pressure on you to quit, you remember this, and it will be your deliverance: I want you to realize that if you are standing on my Word and you are under the most severe attack that you've ever been under, and when there's more pressure on you than you've ever experienced before, that's the time to rejoice. That's a good indication that the devil has just fired his best shot, and if this one doesn't get you, then he's got nothing left. He's finished, and you win."

We don't have to compromise. We don't have to bow. Why bow if you know no weapon that is formed against you shall prosper? Why bow if you know nothing can separate you from the love of God? Why bow if greater is He that is in you than He that is in the world? Why bow if your faith can overcome the world? Why bow if you can do all things through Christ who strengthens you? There's no need to bow. There is no need to compromise.

These three Hebrew men made up their minds. "We are not going to bow. We know our God is able to deliver us." The reason they wouldn't compromise was because they knew God. They didn't just know of Him. They knew how God operated. They knew His delivering power. So they didn't budge when the furious king insulted them by saying, "What God is going to save you?" They instead responded, "We are not careful to answer thee in this matter. *If it be so,* our God whom we serve is able to deliver us from the burning fiery furnace, and he will deliver us out of thine hand, O king" (Dan. 3:16-17, *KJV,* emphasis added). They didn't even have to think about it. They didn't huddle around each other to discuss the matter. They said, "This is the way it is; so do whatever you are going to do, and our God is able to deliver us. We're telling you right now, King, we are not going to bow and we are not going to burn either."

I want you to know that no one had ever talked to King Nebuchadnezzar that way. And most people don't talk to the devil that way either. That's why it shocks him from time to time when somebody who has been programmed by religious tradition all of a sudden gets full of the Word of God and launches an attack on him that he didn't plan on. It's time for you to surprise him. Stand up to him. Let him know that you aren't going to back down this time.

The devil is not the powerful lion he would like you to believe that he is. Like Charles Capps says, "Even if he was a lion, he's got no teeth. Jesus pulled them out in the pit of hell."

The message I want you to get today is that not only is God able, but he *will.* Half the Church today is running around saying, "Our God is able, but you just never know what He will do." If one of those three men had thought that way, they would have burned to death. But those men knew that God was able, and that He *was* going to deliver them out of that fiery furnace.

After these three men said what they said to King Nebuchadnezzar, he became furious. He commanded the guards to turn up the heat seven times greater. That furnace was so hot that the men who threw them in were instantly consumed by the flames. But it did not consume the three young men who knew their God. Why? Because the God who was able to deliver them had already begun to work.

> So Shadrach, Meshach, and Abednego, securely tied, fell into the roaring flames. But suddenly, as he was watching, Nebuchadnezzar jumped up in amazement and exclaimed to his advisers, "Didn't we tie up three men and throw them into the furnace?" "Yes," they said, "we did indeed, Your Majesty." "Look!" Nebuchadnezzar shouted. "I see four men, unbound, walking around in the fire. They aren't even hurt by the flames! And the fourth looks like a divine being!" (Dan. 3:23-25, *NLT*).

They wouldn't compromise God's Word. They knew that if they obeyed God and kept His commandments (the most important for them being "Do not serve other gods before Me"), then God promised them He would conquer their enemies. He had promised that if they were attacked from one direction, then God would scatter them in seven directions (see Deut. 23). Shadrach, Meshach and Abednego stood on their covenant with the Lord and trusted in Him. So what happened? The Fourth Man showed up!

The Fourth Man

Who was the Fourth Man? Let me tell you about Him.

In Genesis He is the seed of woman.

In Exodus He is the Passover lamb.

In Leviticus He is the high priest.

In Numbers He is the pillar of cloud by day and the pillar of fire by night.

In Deuteronomy He is a prophet likened to Moses.

In Joshua He is the captain of our salvation.

In Judges He is the judge and lawgiver.

In Ruth He is our kinsman-redeemer.

In First and Second Samuel He is our trusted prophet.

In First and Second Kings and Chronicles He is the reigning king.

In Ezra He is the faithful scribe.

In Nehemiah He is the rebuilder of broken-down walls of human life.

In Esther He is our Mordecai.

In Job He is our ever-living redeemer.

In Psalms He is our Shepherd.

In Proverbs and Ecclesiastes He is our wisdom.

In the Song of Solomon He is our lover and our bridegroom.

In Isaiah He is the Prince of peace.

In Jeremiah He is the righteous branch.

In Lamentations He is the weeping prophet.

In Ezekiel He is the wonderful four-faced man.

In Daniel He is the Fourth Man in life's fiery furnace.

In Hosea He is the faithful husband.

In Joel He is the baptizer with the Holy Ghost and fire.

In Amos He is our burden-bearer.

In Obadiah He is mighty to save.

In Jonah He is our great foreign missionary.

In Micah He is the messenger with beautiful feet.

In Nahum He is the avenger of God's elect.

In Habakkuk He is God's evangelist.

In Zephaniah He is our savior.

In Haggai He is the restorer of God's lost heritage.

In Zechariah He is the fountain in the house of David for sin and uncleanness.

In Malachi He is the son of righteousness with healing in His wings.

In Matthew He is the Messiah.

In Mark He is the wonder worker.

In Luke He is the Son of Man.

In John He is the Son of God.

In Acts He is the Holy Ghost.

In Romans He is our justifier.

In First and Second Corinthians He is our sanctifier.

In Galatians He is the redeemer from the curse of the law.

In Ephesians He is the Christ with unsearchable riches.

In Philippians He is the God who supplies all of our need.

In Colossians He is the fullness of the Godhead bodily.

In First and Second Thessalonians He is our soon and coming King.

In First and Second Timothy He is the mediator between God and man.

In Titus He is our faithful pastor.

In Philemon He is the beloved brother.

In Hebrews He is the blood and everlasting covenant.

In James He is the great physician.

In First and Second Peter He is the chief shepherd.

In First, Second and Third John He is love.

In Jude He is the Lord Jesus coming with 10,000 of his saints.

In Revelation He is the King of kings and the Lord of lords.

Who is this Fourth Man?

He is Abel's sacrifice.

He is Noah's rainbow.

He is Abraham's ram.

He is Isaac's well.

He is Jacob's scepter.

He is Moses' rod.

He is Joshua's sun and moon that stood still.

He is Elijah's mantle.

He is Elisha's staff.

He is Gideon's fleece.

He is Samuel's horn of oil.

He is David's slingshot.

He is Hezekiah's sundial.

He is Daniel's vision.

He is Amos's burden.

He is Malachi's sun of righteousness.

He is Peter's shadow.

He is Stephen's signs and wonders.

He is Paul's handkerchief and aprons.

He is John's pearly white city.

He is father to the orphan.

He is the husband to the widow.

He is the bright and morning star to the traveler in the night.

He is the lily of the valley.

He is the rose of Sharon.

He is the honey in the rock.

He is the brightness of God's glory.

He is the express image of the person of God.

He is the pearl of great price.

He is the rock in a weary land.

He is the cup that runneth over.

He is the rod and staff that comfort.[1]

Who is this Fourth Man? He is Jesus of Nazareth, the Son of the living God.

If the Son of the living God is not enough to get you over and out of your desperate situation, then there isn't any hope. Jesus is all that you need. Don't bow. Don't compromise. Don't sway to the left or to the right. Keep standing, and know that God is able and He will see you through.

Note

1. Taken by permission from an Oral Roberts sermon preached at a tent revival in 1957.

THE LAW OF PROGRESSION

When you were born again, it was your spirit-man that was recreated. However, you probably didn't immediately change your thinking. You didn't instantly become mature in the things of God. It took some time. In fact, I like to call it the law of progression. When a baby is born into this world, the law of progression is at work in that child. Over time, a baby learns to talk, walk, and then begins to grow in all areas of his or her life. This is the law of progression.

The law of progression works even in the spirit realm. Peter wrote, "You must crave pure spiritual milk so that you can grow into the fullness of your salvation" (1 Pet. 2:2, *NLT*). Paul wrote, "Solid food is for those who are mature, who have trained themselves to recognize the difference between right and wrong and then do what is right" (Heb. 5:14, *NLT*). God wants us to get off of the spiritual bottle. In the natural realm, a child doesn't stay on the bottle its entire life. The same thing applies in the spiritual realm.

As we begin to grow in Christ, it is the meat of God's Word that is going to bring about maturity in our lives. You will never get to the place in your Christian life where you no longer need to read God's Word. You will always need it to be transformed to the image of Jesus.

> But we all, with open face beholding as in a glass the glory of the Lord, are changed into the same image from glory to glory, even as by the Spirit of the Lord (2 Cor. 3:18, *KJV*).

> And all of us, as with unveiled face, [because we] continued to behold [in the Word of God] as in a mirror the

glory of the Lord, are constantly being transfigured into His very own image in ever increasing splendor and from one degree of glory to another; [for this comes] from the Lord [Who is] the Spirit (2 Cor. 3:18, *AMP*).

Paul explained that we are being transformed into the image of God's Son. God's Word acts as a mirror. When we look into the mirror of God's Word, it will reflect an image; and that image is God's image of how He sees you. In other words, God's Word imparted into your heart is going to change you into the image of Jesus Christ. This doesn't happen overnight, of course. You can't pick up your Bible one day and, by the next morning, expect to be made into the image of God's Son. It's a process.

We are being transformed into the image of God's Son. God's Word imparted into your heart is going to change you into the image of Jesus Christ.

Jesus said to His disciples, "You are truly my disciples if you keep obeying my teachings. And you will know the truth, and the truth will set you free" (John 8:31-32, *NLT*). What Jesus was saying was that being made free is a progressive thing. The more of the Truth that we learn, the more free we will be. In the spirit realm, the law of the spirit of life in Jesus has made us free from the law of sin and death. We are free from Satan in the spirit realm. We are free from bondage in the spirit realm. But as we continue in the Word, we will become freer in the natural realm.

The definition of progression is to move forward or onward. It means development. It means improvement. It means to continue toward completion. If God tells you to do something, then you can't stop until it's completed. If you do, then you won't be rewarded. Refuse to back off until whatever God wants you to do is accomplished.

The law of progression relates to the faith walk. Stability in faith comes as a result of standing on God's Word. That is, stability comes when you keep on believing, even though you see nothing happening. Many have become discouraged, sidetracked and beaten down because, after they've prayed and stood in faith and nothing seems to be happening, they fall back. They withdraw and consider it a bad experience. But something *is* happening. There is a law at work, the law of progression. Yet you can negate that law by drawing back. You can stop the law of progression.

All of nature functions on this law. Jesus said, "This is what the kingdom of God is like. A man scatters seed on the ground. Night and day, whether he sleeps or gets up, the seed sprouts and grows, though he does not know how. All by itself the soil produces grain—first the stalk, then the head, then the full kernel in the head. As soon as the grain is ripe, he puts the sickle to it, because the harvest has come" (Mark 4:26-29, *NIV*).

Look at the law of progression at work here. The harvest does not come in one step. You don't put a seed in the ground and then expect it to become a stalk overnight. Jesus mentioned several steps in that passage after the seed is planted. First, the leaf blade pushes through. Second, the heads form. Third, the grain ripens.

Then it's time to harvest. Jesus said that is how the kingdom of God operates.

When you begin to make your application of faith, and you begin to say what God's Word says, you are like that farmer planting a seed into the ground. Once you speak forth that word, it is going to be your responsibility to protect it just like it is the responsibility of the farmer to protect that seed. Don't let weeds grow up around it. Don't allow doubt and unbelief to gather up around it. Don't let anything destroy that seed before it has opportunity to take root and grow. You are going to have to stand guard over the seed. You are going to have to stand guard over the Word. You are going to have to stand guard over your faith.

I remember that when my daughters were young, I bought them some little chicks to raise. My girls loved them. Soon we had a bunch of hens running around, so I built a little coop for them. A friend of mine gave me a rooster. I thought it would be exciting for my girls to see how eggs turn into chicks. So before long, one of our hens was laying eggs. I could hardly wait for the first chick to hatch. I'd sit out there night after night waiting for them to hatch. Nothing was happening.

But then one day, when I was feeding them and was just about to walk away, I looked down and saw an egg moving around. I couldn't believe it. I was so excited. I ran inside the house, grabbed my girls and showed them what was going on. They saw the first crack in that egg and watched until the little chick was hatched.

I want you to know that if you let the law of progression work and not negate it, there will come a time when it will produce results. You are going to see a blade come up. It might take some time, but be willing to wait for it. Stay patient and single-minded, and before long, you will see that the law of progression really works.

"This is what the kingdom of God is like. A man scatters seed on the ground. Night and day, whether he sleeps or gets up, the seed sprouts and grows, though he does not know how" (Mark 4:26-27, *NIV*). This is important. This farmer has total trust in the seed. He plants it in the ground and goes to bed. Once the seed is in the ground, it's beyond his control at that point. He doesn't know how it's all going to work. He believes the seed will do what it is designed to do, and he doesn't get discouraged in the meanwhile.

I'm reminded of what someone told me once. She said, "Brother Jerry, I've confessed the Word three times, and nothing's happened." I replied, "Boy, you really hung in there, didn't you? Wow! You confessed three times. That's perseverance." I was being sarcastic, of course, but I was trying to make the point that that is not what the life of faith is about. The life of faith is not a two-week experience and then you give up if it doesn't seem to work. It's a way of life.

You can't see what the word, or that seed, is doing in the spirit realm. Our church is in a building program right now. We are constructing new facilities, and the Lord told me that we wouldn't have to borrow any money for them.

I'll be honest, sometimes it has been tight, especially considering the huge general operating expenses we have in addition to building new buildings. Often, I couldn't figure out how the money was going to come in. But we've stood firm and believed God, and we've received. We had to keep the wheels of progress turning.

If you let the law of progression work, it will produce results. Stay patient and singleminded, and before long, you will see that the law of progression really works.

Some time ago, the Spirit of God spoke to me and told me to put $5,000 into a particular ministry. I wrote the check and gave it to the minister. Five thousand dollars is a lot of money. I could have used that money for plenty of things—our building project for one. But God gave me a task and I did it. What I didn't know was that that very day, God spoke to a man out in California and told him to write a check for $10,000 to our ministry. And it came in at the exact time we needed it. I didn't know what was happening behind the scenes. I just believed that the seed I sowed was going to do its job.

One Step at a Time

"The steps of a good man are ordered by the LORD" (Ps. 37:23, *KJV*). What does this mean? I've had people tell me they are tired of hearing me teaching about "all them steps." Seven steps to this, four steps to that. But that's how God deals with us. He deals with most of us in steps.

A lot of people are not willing to take steps. A lot of people ignore steps. A lot of people think they don't need steps. That's why a lot of Christians are fumbling through life. They disregard God's ordered steps. In the natural mind it may make sense to jump from one point to another instead of taking smaller steps. We might think we'll get somewhere faster or it would be more fun or it would save us some time. But if we jump instead of step, what's going to happen? We might get hurt. We could stumble. We could fall; and then we're going to get discouraged. And that will prolong the manifestation.

Every step we take gets us closer to our manifestation. That is what the law of progression is all about. We keep moving forward. We gain momentum. We take step after step until it happens. The name of the game is winning. It's not how long it takes or how fast we can get there. It's all about winning and living a victorious life.

Let God be the navigator of the steps you take in your life. If you'll just be obedient, then you'll end up where God wants you to be.

Let Patience Be Perfected

Continue to listen to God and don't get sidetracked. Don't be like the children of Israel and wander around in circles for 40 years. They could have crossed that desert in 40 days, but because they weren't willing to obey God, it took them 40 years.

Many Christians do the same thing. They feel strong in the Lord on Sunday, but by Wednesday, they're saying things like, "This faith stuff doesn't work." You have to be single-minded in order for the law of progression to work for you. You can't be looking for excuses to give up.

"Count it all joy when ye fall into divers temptations; Knowing this, that the trying of your faith worketh patience. But let patience have her perfect work, that ye may be perfect and entire, wanting nothing" (Jas. 1:2-4, *KJV*). James told us to be patient so that it could have her "perfect work." Patience works hand in hand with the law of progression.

When you are standing on the authority of God's Word, there are opportunities for you to cast your faith aside. There are opportunities for you to draw back. There are opportunities for you to give up. But you have to remain patient. You start out by confessing God's Word. You believe; you receive. You act on the Word. You continually feed your spirit. You remain constant and add patience to your faith. The Bible says that if you let patience have her perfect work, you will want for nothing.

When Carolyn and I first made the decision to live by God's Word, it was obvious that we needed everything. My business was deep in debt. Our finances were a wreck. We had moved to Forth Worth, Texas, to work with brother Kenneth Copeland, and we didn't even know where we were going to live. We finally moved into a little dump and barely had the money to pay for utilities, groceries and a few other things that we needed to get by.

Carolyn and I were believing God for all the needs we had. The first thing we needed to believe God for was a better car. I knew someone who owned a 1969 Pontiac Bonneville who told me, "Jerry, I am going to sell that car to you. I believe God wants you to have it. You've been in the automotive business, so you know what the car is worth. But God told me to sell it to you for

$1,200." I knew the car was definitely worth a whole lot more than that. So Carolyn and I prayed, and the Spirit of God revealed to us that this car belonged to us.

I told the man we definitely wanted the car, and he asked how I was going to handle the financial arrangement. I said, "Will Mark 11:24 do?" I didn't have a penny to my name. He said, "Sure, I agree with that. In the name of Jesus, I believe this car is yours. When the money comes in, let me know." Some time went by, and it didn't look like any money would be coming in for that car any time soon.

Every few weeks he'd call me and ask, "Jerry, did you get the money yet?" And every time I told him, "According to Mark 11:24, I believe I will receive it." Finally, he called me one day and said, "Jerry, it really hurts me to have to tell you this. I'm going to have to sell the car, and I just can't wait anymore." Talk about the devil jumping on me. I heard him whisper in my ear, "I told you you'd never get that car."

There was a long silence on the phone. I prayed, *God, if this faith thing doesn't work on the car that I need, there is no way I can ever believe it will work on anything else.* I finally told the man, "You do whatever you need to do," and I hung up the phone. This situation shook me up pretty bad. It was jeopardizing my faith. I realized I needed some wisdom, and the Spirit of God told me to turn to the book of James.

I started reading, "Count it all joy when ye fall into divers temptations . . ." (1:2, *KJV*), and thought, "You've got to be kidding me! I'm supposed to lift my hands, praise God and hoop and holler because I didn't get my car?" The Holy Spirit kept prompting me to read it over and over until I got what He was trying to teach me.

Finally, I got to the part where it read, "that the trying of your faith worketh patience . . . let patience have her perfect work." Patience? I didn't need patience. I needed a car. However, God taught me a great lesson that day.

I thought patience meant you just put up with whatever you have to put up with and hope to God that one day it will get better. I was wrong. God told me that was not patience. "Every good gift and every perfect gift is from above, and cometh down from the Father of lights, with whom is no variableness, neither shadow of turning" (Jas. 1:17, *KJV*). God told me that this is patience. It means consistency. No "shadow of turning." He told me to keep meditating on that passage of Scripture. "If any of you lack wisdom, let him ask of God, that giveth to all men liberally, and upbraideth not; and it shall be given him. But let him ask in faith, nothing wavering. For he that wavereth is like a wave of the sea driven with the wind and tossed. For let not that man think that he shall receive any thing of the Lord. A double minded man is unstable in all his ways" (Jas. 1:5-8, *KJV*).

The Lord kept repeating, "A doubleminded man is unstable in all his ways." I thought of the man who told me that he needed to sell that car, and I asked God, "Are you trying to tell me the car is still mine? Because if You remember, he said he was going to sell it!" Once again I kept thinking of the sentence, "A double-minded man is unstable in all his ways." God spoke to me, "I wouldn't have told you in the beginning that it was your car if it wasn't. It would be different if you were going out there just trying to make something happen on your own. But I've been ordering your steps, and I'm the one who told you that this is your car."

I had my revelation. I jumped up and ran to find my wife. "Carolyn, the man called and he said he was going to sell our car. But I'm not moved by what I hear. God said it's ours, and I'm not going to let it go. Whoever buys it will just have to give it to us. It's our car." You would have thought that after a super-revelation like that, the car would have shown up that very moment. Nope. But two weeks later I got a phone call from that same man. "Jerry," he said. "You know how I told you I was going to sell that car? It's a funny thing. After we finished our conversation, I told one of my employees to go sell it. 'Well' he said, 'I don't want to do that. That's Jerry's car, and you know it.'" The law of progression was at work.

A few weeks went by and I was invited to preach in a meeting in Arkansas. As I got ready to leave, the man called me and said he didn't want me traveling on the road with the old clunker I had, and he wanted me to drive the 1969 Pontiac. "I know the money will come," he told me. When we got back from Arkansas, guess what happened? Someone went to the man and gave him a check for $1,200 and paid my car off for me!

I don't know how it happened. I don't know who it was. All I know is that it worked. The law of progression worked! While I was standing on the authority of God's Word . . . while I was taking one step at a time . . . while I was being patient and single-minded . . . while I was doing exactly what God told me to do . . . I was getting closer and closer to the manifestation. Once you start moving out into your faith endeavor, you owe it to yourself to let the law of progression work for you until you move right into completion.

The Enemy of Progression

"Be not deceived; God is not mocked: for whatsoever a man soweth, that shall he also reap. For he that soweth to his flesh shall of the flesh reap corruption; but he that soweth to the Spirit shall of the Spirit reap life everlasting. And let us not be weary in well doing: for in due season we shall reap, if we faint not" (Gal. 6:7-9, *KJV*). God presents us with a condition in these verses. If we don't faint, we reap. If we faint, we don't reap.

One of the major enemies of progress is weariness. Fainting stops progress. Some people get tired of confessing the Word. Some people get tired of acting on the Word. Some people get tired of giving. Some people get tired of praying. Some people get tired of believing. Why? Because it looks like their confession is not bringing possession. And they go to the next logical thing to do in the natural. They get discouraged and weary. Do you know what that does? That stops the wheels of progression.

People who accomplish great things are a highly motivated and untiring people. It seems like they have more stamina than everyone else. I want you to know that if you keep feeding on the Word of God, you can become a person like this. You will be motivated through every trial, every valley, every hard place and every crisis. If you stand uncompromisingly, you will appear to others as untiring and full of spunk.

Cast not away therefore your confidence, which hath great recompence of reward. For ye have need of patience, that, after ye have done the will of God, ye might receive the promise. For yet a little while, and he that shall come will come, and will not tarry. Now the just shall live by faith: but if any man draw back, my soul shall have no pleasure in him (Heb. 10:35-38, *KJV*).

But without faith it is impossible to please him: for he that cometh to God must believe that he is, and that he is a rewarder of them that diligently seek him (Heb. 11:6, *KJV*).

God doesn't reward those who become weary. God doesn't reward those who are slothful. God doesn't reward those who have a spirit of lethargy. He is a rewarder of those who diligently seek Him. The blessings come to the doers, not the tryers and the quitters.

"Now the just shall live by faith: but if any man draws back, my soul shall have no pleasure in him." We know that God loves you whether you draw back or not. It's not a question of His love. What the Bible says is that He has no "pleasure" in those who draw back. It grieves God when He sees us constantly being run over by the devil, especially after what He has invested into our lives. Especially after He imparted the measure of faith into our hearts. Especially after He created us to overcome and pull down strongholds. God gets excited and takes pleasure in us winning!

Why would any man or woman draw back when he or she is progressing? It doesn't make sense. It can only be because they got discouraged, became weary or have fainted.

Remember, if we faint not, we shall reap. We need to keep our faith up against the mountain until it has been removed. That's progression.

You may be in an impossible-looking situation. Perhaps you are in a transition period. You need a job. You need healing. You need unity in your family. You need a financial breakthrough. You have been standing on the authority of God's Word, believing God to order your steps, and it seems like every step you've taken has resulted in a closed door.

I want to remind you of something that happened in Jesus' ministry. In Mark, we read how Jesus was preaching in a house in Capernaum. The place was packed, and no more people could get in. A couple of men came carrying one of their friends on a mat. This man had palsy and wanted to be healed by Jesus, but there was no room for him to get through. I like to say the door was closed! One translation tells us these men sought "means" to get to Jesus. That implies that when every door was shut, they kept on moving forward. They didn't give up. They kept moving forward.

In the natural, it seemed there was no way to get the man with palsy into the physical presence of Jesus. But these guys kept seeking out a "means" to do so. Finally, they tore off the roof and lowered him down into the room. When there appeared to be no way, there was a way. After reading this passage one day, God told me I had to be willing to "raise the roof." Never settle for "no." I had to keep seeking a means to get through.

Don't misunderstand me, I'm not telling you to go and tear somebody's roof off. I'm just saying don't get weary. Don't give up. Don't get discouraged. Don't compromise. Don't omit. Let the law of progression work in your situation and you will see the Word of God come to completion.

11

A PATH RUNS THROUGH IT

What Happens Behind the Scenes

Many years ago, I watched the movie *A River Runs Through It*. It's about two brothers who grow up with a very strict father. The only real enjoyment they had as kids was learning the art of trout fishing with their dad. A few weeks after I saw this movie, I was meditating on Psalm 77, and it reminded me of the film. It also reminded me of a powerful principle I want to share with you.

> You are the God of miracles and wonders! You demonstrate your awesome power among the nations. You have redeemed your people by your strength, the descendants of Jacob and of Joseph by your might. When the Red Sea saw you, O God, its waters looked and trembled! The sea quaked to its very depths. The clouds poured down their rain; the thunder rolled and crackled in the sky. Your arrows of lightning flashed. Your thunder roared from the whirlwind; the lightning lit up the world! The earth trembled and shook. *Your road led through the sea, your pathway through the mighty waters—a pathway no one knew was there!* You led your people along that road like a flock of sheep, with Moses and Aaron as their shepherds (Ps. 77:14-20, *NLT*, emphasis added).

Notice that God created a path in the middle of a great sea. This Scripture is a reference to the Exodus story, of how God delivered the nation of Israel from the Egyptians. It is specifically talking about the parting of the Red Sea—the pathway was there all along, but no one knew of it. There is a path that is running through every adversity you are encountering at this very moment in your life. No matter what kind of obstacle you may be facing, no matter what kind of barriers you may be confronted with, no matter what kind of walls may be standing between you and victory, know that a path runs through it.

What this psalm tells me is that God is always working behind the scenes. He is working on our behalf even when we can't see anything happening; even when we can't feel anything; and even when it looks the darkest. The idea of God working behind the scenes has been a revelation to me for many, many years. If I did not believe that every time I face an impossible-looking situation that God was working behind the scenes, I would not be able to endure them. I would not be able to persevere. I would have no drive. I would have no motivation. Knowing that God is working on my behalf, whether or not I can see or feel it, is what has kept me going during the times when it looked like I couldn't go any further.

As Pharaoh and his army approached, the people of Israel could see them in the distance, marching toward them. The people began to panic, and they cried out to the LORD for help. Then they turned against Moses and complained, "Why did you bring us out here to die in the wilderness? Weren't there enough graves for us in Egypt? Why did you make us leave? Didn't we tell you to leave us alone while we were still in Egypt? Our Egyptian slavery was far better than dying out here in the wilderness!" (Exod. 14:10-12, *NLT*).

This is the same group of people that had been begging God for deliverance when they were in bondage in the land of Egypt. They cried out to God and He sent them a leader, Moses. They didn't like Moses, however, because he didn't handle their deliverance as they would have liked. Though they walked out of Egypt free people, carrying the gold and silver of their enemy, they soon came face to face with the Red Sea. In their minds at that point, it looked as though it was all over. It looked as though Moses had led them straight into defeat.

No matter what kind of obstacle you may be facing or barriers you are confronted with or walls that may be standing between you and victory, a path runs through it.

I'm sure you have reached a place at some point in your life where it looked as though it was all over. If we're honest with ourselves, most of us have. Many years ago, I had the devil say to me, "It's been a nice ride, Jerry, but this is as far as you're going." Though I replied, "Says who?" I admit I entertained that thought for a few moments. It reminds me of a story I heard about brother Kenneth Hagin. A woman once came up to him and asked him to pray for her so that she would never have another negative thought. Brother Hagin told her, "Miss, if I could pray that for you, I'd pray it for myself." All of us are vulnerable to negative thoughts, but the important thing is that we don't dwell on negativity. We need to learn how to cast down negative thoughts.

The Israelites were in an impossible-looking situation. As the popular saying goes, they were between a rock and a hard place. They couldn't turn back because Pharaoh was either going to kill them or take them back into captivity. They couldn't go forward because there was a Red Sea in front of them. In the natural it looked to them that all Moses did was stir them up and build up their hopes only to let them down. In their minds, they thought it was all over.

You have to remember that they didn't know that God had the power to split seas. They'd never seen Him do it. They didn't have the book of Exodus to read. They were *living* their exodus. Not one of them said, "Oh, wait a minute. I think I see a path running through the Red Sea." Why? Because the Bible said it was a pathway that no one knew was there.

It had been there for quite some time. In the same way, the path that God sets for your life is already there as well. Do you know that God knows everything about your life? Do you know that He knows everything that you will go through from now until you get to heaven? God is never surprised by anything that happens to you. The Bible even says that He gives you the guarantee that He will not allow Satan to put you through anything in your life that you are not able to bear. Whatever you are going through right now, God has already determined you've got what it takes to make it through. You are able to endure it, persevere through it and come out on the other side victorious.

A few years after I watched the movie *The Right Stuff,* in the early eighties, I went to the Indy 500 and had the privilege of sitting next to Colonel Chuck Yeager on the flight there. He was to be the driver for the Pace car at the Indy that year. If you know anything about this man, you know he was the first person to break the sound barrier. His story is told in that movie. It was a pleasure to sit next to someone who had the "right stuff." Because of God, you and I have the right stuff.

"But Moses told the people, 'Don't be afraid. Just stand where you are and watch the LORD rescue you. The Egyptians that you see today will never be seen again. The LORD himself will fight for you'" (Exod. 14:13-14, *NLT*). Moses' advice to the people was easier said than done, but it's an important lesson to learn. What do most people do when they are going through something that looks impossible? They do the opposite of holding their peace. They panic. They start griping and moaning and whining and complaining and sobbing and bawling. Have you ever tried to talk to someone who is in panic stage? It's almost impossible to calm him down.

This is what the people of Israel were like when they stared at that Red Sea in front of them. But God was saying, "You watch. I'm up to something. I've been working behind the scenes. I've had something prepared since you were crying out to Me for deliverance a long time ago. I already had a path created for you through this Red Sea."

I think it's interesting that the Israelites' very problem became their answer. Could it be that the very thing you are going through right now could turn out to be your solution? You might be going through a tremendous financial attack. Well, that could mean you are about to experience your greatest financial breakthrough! Great victories come out of great battles. But the people of God couldn't see this. All they could see was a Red Sea (just like all you can see right now in your life is a mountain of debt or the strife in your family or the job that you lost).

Just Keep Moving

Moses had sense enough to believe what God had told him even though he didn't know that there was a path in the middle of the Red Sea. God asked Moses, "Why are you crying out to me? Tell the people to get moving!" (Exod. 14:15, *NLT*). Another translation tells us that God told Moses to tell the people to "go forward." God's direction for your life is to always go forward. It might seem like all you are doing is taking a baby step, but that is still forward motion. God didn't tell the people of Israel to retreat. He commanded them to move on and then said to Moses:

> Use your shepherd's staff—hold it out over the water, and a path will open up before you through the sea. Then all the people of Israel will walk through on dry ground. Yet I will harden the hearts of the Egyptians, and they will follow the Israelites into the sea. Then I will receive great glory at the expense of Pharaoh and his armies, chariots, and charioteers. When I am finished with Pharaoh and his army, all Egypt will know that I am the LORD! (Exod. 14:16-18, *NLT*).

We all know what happened after that. The Red Sea parted and the Israelites walked right on through while the Egyptian army behind them was swallowed by the sea. "Your road led through the sea, your pathway through the mighty waters" (Ps. 77:19, *NLT*).

In order for those people to find the path that no one could see, they had to be *willing to obey*. They had to take a step of faith. How would you like to have been the person on the front line? The people of Israel were about three million in number, and the ones in the back possibly hadn't even seen the Red Sea yet. They didn't know it was in front of them. So they were back there shaking their tambourines and praising God that they had been delivered from Egypt, while the ones in the front were staring at the rushing waters saying, "We're gonna die. We're gonna die." But Moses took a leap of faith and obeyed God. And the people took a leap of faith, trusted in what God had to say through Moses and went forward in obedience.

In order for the Israelites to find the path that no one could see, they had to be willing to obey. They took a leap of faith, trusted in what God had to say through Moses and went forward in obedience.

You may be looking at your Red Sea right now, wondering what you are going to do. I'll tell you! Move forward. Sometimes the only move "forward" is to get in your prayer closet, cast those negative thoughts out of your mind and start praising God. If you stop going to church when your life is full of adversity, you are not going forward. If you hang around negative people who say they tried it and it didn't work for them, you are not going forward. You've got to hang around some winners. Get around those who have the right stuff. Get around some people who know there is a path that runs through your situation.

The devil is good at getting us to say things that bind us, limit us, restrict us and trap us. "Thou art snared with the words of thy mouth" (Prov. 6:2, *KJV*). Satan has convinced us to say, "I can't see any way out of this." There has never been a more devil-inspired statement come out of the mouth of a believer than that one.

I heard somebody say, "I can't believe something if I can't see it." When God says there is a path that runs through it, of course you can't see it. But since when do we govern our lives by what we can see? We walk by faith, not by sight. We don't have to see a path to believe it's there. Do you believe you have a brain? Of course. Can you see your brain? Of course not. So, we *can* believe things that we cannot see.

I travel quite a lot, and often without my wife, because she doesn't like the kind of hectic traveling I do. People often ask me if I'm married, because they don't see Carolyn that much. Some of them even wonder if she exists! But she does, and I'm married, and just because they can't see her doesn't mean that she doesn't exist.

You've got to believe deep down in your spirit that there is a path. You've got to be convinced of this no matter what you are going through, and especially no matter how many people try to discourage you just because they never found their path. Contrary to what happened to them, and contrary to your past experiences, you've got to believe that somehow, someway, no matter what you're going through right now, a path is running through it. A path is running through your adversity. A path is running through every test and every trial. A path is running through every impossible-looking situation.

I can tell you that over the last 40 years, God has never let me down. There were times I thought He might have been late, but in reality He was always on time. He's always created paths right through the middle of every challenge I have ever experienced. God is no respecter of persons, so I know He is doing the same for you right now.

The Holy Spirit, Our Helper

If you are ever going to discover this path, you are going to have to learn to be sensitive to the leading of the Holy Spirit. Jesus said, "I will not leave you comfortless: I will come to you" (John 14:18, *KJV*) or "I will not leave you as orphans [comfortless, desolate, bereaved, forlorn, helpless]; I will come [back] to you" (*AMP*). He was talking about sending the Holy Spirit who would act as our helper. In John 16:33, Jesus referred to the Holy Spirit as our guide. What is the major characteristic of a guide? A guide knows the way; he knows things you don't know. You don't hire a person to be a guide if he doesn't know where he is going. I am not going through the Grand Canyon with somebody who's never been through the Grand Canyon before.

I took my daughters to Africa with me some years back. We traveled to Botswana for the graduation celebrations in our Bible schools, and we preached in a couple of our churches there. One of our partners blessed us by giving us a safari trip. We were assigned two guides—Richard and Job. (I got a little concerned when I found out the one guy's name was Job, but he turned out to be a remarkable man and an amazing guide.)

We were given a Range Rover to ride around in, and while Richard drove, Job sat on a chair outside, above the hood, so he could see everything and tell us about it. We went out at different times during the day, sometimes in the mornings, sometimes during the evenings. Job knew everything there was to know. He showed us all sorts of wild animals and explained their activities.

A path is running through your adversity.
A path is running through every test and every trial.
If you are ever going to discover this path, you have to learn
to be sensitive to the leading of the Holy Spirit.

It was like he was a part of the environment. He smelled things we couldn't smell. He heard things we couldn't hear. He saw things we couldn't see. One time, we were driving around just before it got dark, and all of a sudden, as we were waiting for Job to tell us what was coming up next, he calmly said, "Snake." He didn't yell it out; he said it very matter-of-factly. Wouldn't you know it, right above our heads, in a tree, we saw a snake slithering around.

What's my point? Job knew the way. He knew more than we knew. He had the characteristics of a great guide. If anybody knows where the path is in the middle of our dire circumstances, it's the Holy Spirit. That's the reason God filled us with the Holy Spirit. Not so that we could be called Pentecostal or tongue-talkers, but so that we would have a Guide. He wants to lead us to the path to victory, the path to the good life. The path to increase. The path to the barriers coming down. The path to doors being opened. The path to the goodness of God. The path to God's best. The path to everything God wants us to have.

"No one can know what anyone else is really thinking except that person alone, and no one can know God's thoughts except God's own Spirit. And God has actually given us his Spirit (not the world's spirit) so we can know the wonderful things God has freely given us" (1 Cor. 2:11-12, *NLT*). *THE MESSAGE* tells us that the Spirit "brings out what God planned all along" (v. 10). Isn't that encouraging? One of the jobs of the Holy Spirit is to bring out or reveal what God had planned for you all along. He knows where that path is. He knows how to get you on that path. It's His job to bring it out, but you have got to give Him some time. You've got to learn to be sensitive to Him.

Exodus 14:30 tells us, "The LORD saved Israel that day" (*KJV*). That's what He wants to do for you and me. He wants us to have the testimony that He saved us, delivered us and brought us through to victory. Learn to line up your words and your thoughts with what God says. Don't focus on the circumstances; focus on fellowshipping with the Holy Spirit and endeavoring to be sensitive to His leadership. Ask Him to reveal to you God's plan. Ask Him to reveal to you the path to your victory. If you don't hear anything while praying and seeking God, don't give up. Keep on listening for Him day after day after day.

Line up your words and your thoughts with what God says. Don't focus on circumstances; focus on fellowshipping with the Holy Spirit and endeavoring to be sensitive to His leadership. Ask Him to reveal to you God's plan.

Let me make another suggestion. Don't ever act out of confusion. God is not the author of confusion. If you are ever confused about going this way or going that way, taking this job or that job, moving here or moving there, then don't act just yet. God is the author of peace. If you do whatever you're going to do out of uncertainty, you are about to make a big mistake. You will make an even bigger mess of your situation. Wait patiently on the Holy Spirit. Wait for peace and then follow it.

Getting Out of the Valley

"Blessed are those whose strength is in you, who have set their hearts on pilgrimage. As they pass through the Valley of Baca, they make it a place of springs; the autumn rains also cover it with pools. They go from strength to strength, till each appears before God in Zion" (Ps. 84:5-7, *NIV*). The literal Hebrew meaning of the words "Valley of Baca" is "the valley of tears" or "the valley of sorrow." When we experience challenges in our life, it can drive us to tears. It can create sorrow. It can make us feel sad and oppressed. Most of us have visited this place several times. The writer of this psalm, however, encourages us by talking of "passing through" the Valley of Baca. The *Amplified Bible* translates this as going "from strength to strength [increasing in victorious power]."

God doesn't want you living in the Valley of Baca. It's not a place to be stayed in for very long. The people who know how to properly visit Baca pass right on through it; and when they come out of it; they are stronger. They come out on the other side increased in victorious power. That's exactly how God wants you to come through. He wants you coming out of that place with strength, power and victory.

I have discovered that when I am in the Valley of Baca, and I can't see God's path, then that's when I need to pray in the Spirit more. You need to do the same thing. When you get up in the morning, pray in the Spirit. While you're getting dressed, pray in the Spirit. Pray in the Spirit during your lunch break. Pray in the Spirit when you are driving to work. Pray in the Spirit when you are taking a shower. Pray in the Spirit when you go to bed. What happens when you do this? You're giving the Holy Spirit an opportunity to reveal to you where that path is.

There's a path running through whatever you are going through today. God has already provided it, but you have to enlist the help of your Guide. You'll have to get some assistance from your Helper. Spend time with the Holy Spirit and you will find the path that runs through your problem, and it will lead you straight to your victory.

12

GOD WILL BE EVERYTHING
YOU NEED

God Is

When you struggle with your faith, the best thing to do is to get back to the basics. You can't get any more basic than studying Hebrews 11, the great life of faith chapter in the Bible. You have to keep your faith fed all the time. You can't live on last year's faith, just like you can't live on yesterday's manna. It has to be fresh manna every day.

"But without faith it is impossible to please him: for he that cometh to God must believe that he is, and that he is a rewarder of them that diligently seek him" (Heb. 11:6, *KJV*). I frequently speak on this verse in the context of perseverance and not giving up ("he is a rewarder of them that diligently seek him"). One day, as I was meditating on this verse, I started to focus on the part that says, "For he that cometh to God must believe that he is." What does this really mean? It means believing more than the simple fact that God exists. It means believing that God is everything we need Him to be in our lives.

What is your need today? What are you battling against? What kind of hurts are you dealing with? What's got you under pressure? What kinds of attacks have come into your life? Whatever they are, know that God is able to meet them all. He is whatever you need Him to be. One of the many names of God is I AM. Not "I was." Not "I have been." Not "I used to be." God is!

This is what He was trying to get across to Moses when He called him to lead the people of Israel out of Egypt. Moses came up with a bunch of excuses why he thought he wasn't the man for the job. "I can't do this. I can't go before Pharaoh and tell him to let Your people go. I can't speak well. I don't have the confidence." But God ignored Moses' whining and said to him, "You just go ahead and tell Pharaoh that I AM has sent you."

The foundational truth for strong faith is believing that "God is." It is only this kind of faith that can move mountains, pull down strongholds, overcome the world and bring about victory. If you want this kind of faith, then you have to be convinced that God is whatever you need Him to be.

God is the great I AM. This is why we find numerous references throughout the Bible of the names that people gave God once they discovered that He could be everything they needed Him to be. King David was famous for this. Among many others names, he referred to God as his Refuge, High Tower, Deliverer, Comforter and Fortress. That is who David found God to be during his times of trouble and distress. If David needed God to be a refuge, God said: "I AM." If David needed God to be a protector, God said: "I AM." If David needed God to be a comforter, God said: "I AM." And God is saying the same thing to you and me today. Whatever you need in your life, God is saying: "I AM."

One of the many names for God is I AM. Not "I was."
Not "I have been." Not "I used to be."
Whatever you need in your life, God is saying: "I AM."

When David referred to God as his refuge or his fortress, he was writing from personal experience. The names he attributed to God were not just a simple description, something deeply meaningful and personal. God wasn't just a refuge; He was David's refuge. God wasn't just a deliverer. God became David's deliverer. The same can be true in your own life. Once you have been healed by God, then He becomes your healer. Once you have been provided for, God becomes your provider. Once you have been comforted, God becomes your comforter. There is a difference between God being "a" something and God being "your" something. When God is "your something," then you have personal experience.

"The LORD is my rock, and my fortress, and my deliverer; my God, my strength, in whom I will trust; my buckler, and the horn of my salvation, and my high tower" (Ps. 18:2, *KJV*). David wrote this psalm while he was fleeing from King Saul and sought refuge in a cave. Saul was an angry, jealous man who was out to kill David; but God delivered David from Saul's evil hands. In writing this passage, David learned seven new things about God, and He gave God seven new names from this experience: God was his Rock, his Fortress, his Deliverer, his Strength, his Buckler, the Horn of his Salvation and his High Tower. These names described what David needed God to be, and God became all of those things.

> The LORD is my shepherd; I have everything I need. He lets me rest in green meadows; he leads me beside peaceful streams. He renews my strength. He guides me along right paths, bringing honor to his name. Even when I walk through the dark valley of death, I will not be afraid, for you are close beside me. Your rod and your staff protect

and comfort me. You prepare a feast for me in the presence of my enemies. You welcome me as a guest, anointing my head with oil. My cup overflows with blessings. Surely your goodness and unfailing love will pursue me all the days of my life, and I will live in the house of the LORD forever (Ps. 23, *NLT*).

Many theologians agree that this most famous psalm was written by an elderly David. It's not the song of a novice, but of a man who had walked with God for many years. David called God his shepherd. In the New Testament, Jesus called us His sheep. This is not a putdown; it's a fact. Let's be honest. Sheep do dumb things. That's why they need a shepherd. Sheep wouldn't know where to go if it wasn't for a shepherd leading them. Sheep would be eaten by wolves if it wasn't for a shepherd taking care of them.

What David was saying here is this: "I'm an old man now; and in my opinion, if you were to ask me what God has been to me all my life, I would say He's my Shepherd. He has led me. He has guided me. He has protected me. Sometimes I messed up, sometimes I was stubborn, sometimes I rebelled, and sometimes I went the wrong way, but God was always there and ready to lead me into His path of righteousness."

Who Is God?

The Bible, from Genesis to Revelation, reveals to us that God is everything we need Him to be. Let me give you some examples of what that means.

In Genesis 15:1, He is our shield.

In Genesis 17:1, He is almighty God or El Shaddai.

In Exodus 15:26, He is the Lord that heals.

In Deuteronomy 5:6, He is the Lord who brought you out of bondage.

In Isaiah 43:3, He is the Lord thy God, the Holy One of Israel, thy Savior.

In Isaiah 48:12, He is the first and the last.

In Isaiah 48:17, He is the God who teaches you to profit.

In Isaiah 51:12, He is the God that comforts you.

In Jeremiah 3:12, He is merciful.

In Jeremiah 9:24, He is the Lord of loving-kindness (or mercy).

In John 6:35, He is the bread of life.

In John 8:12, He is the light of the world.

In John 10:9, He is the door.

In John 10:11, He is the good shepherd.

In John 14:6, He is the way, the truth and the life.

In Revelation 1:8, He is the alpha and the omega.

If you trust and hope in God, He will be whatever you need Him to be. God has the unique ability to fit into every man and every woman's life. God is so much. He is so much that every human being has the ability to relate to Him. No matter who you are, no matter where you were born and no matter what your occupation may be, He is whatever you need Him to be. Many years ago, I heard someone say the following about who

God is. It helped me understand how God fills every need.

To the architect—He is the chief cornerstone.
To the baker—He is the living bread.
To the banker—He is the unsearchable riches.
To the biologist—He is life.
To the builder—He is the sure foundation.
To the doctor—He is the great physician.
To the educator—He is the superb teacher.
To the farmer—He is the Lord of the harvest.
To the florist—He is the rose of Sharon.
To the geologist—He is the rock of ages.
To the jeweler—He is the precious stone.
To the lawyer—He is the counselor and the advocate.
To the media—He is good news and glad tidings.
To the philosopher—He is wisdom.
To the potter—He is the vessel of honor.
To the sailor—He is the master of the sea.
To the soldier—He is the captain of our salvation.
To the statesman—He is the desire of all nations.

God is everything you will ever need Him to be. There is no need greater than our God. There is no circumstance that is too big for God. There is no problem that God can't solve. Whatever your need is, God is.

If, in your mind, your need gets bigger than God, then you are spending too much time listening to the devil. You are allowing him to talk to you too much. You are not casting down his imaginations. Satan wants you to think that whatever you are going through at this present moment is greater than the God you serve, but it is not! You can't be Almighty and then have something that is mightier than you. You can't be Most High and have something that is higher than you. Our God is Almighty and our God is Most High!

The Strong One

The Hebrew prefix "el" means "strong one." In the Old Testament, particularly in the books of Job and Psalms, "el" is used about 250 times. The use of the word indicated specific circumstances that called for God to manifest His great strength or great power. When God's people came up against something they did not have the ability, the might or the strength to deal with themselves, the Strong One showed up. This should encourage all of us today. We are blessed to be children of the Strong One.

When I was a little boy, I thought my dad was the strongest daddy on the planet. As we said in the South, I believed that he could "whoop" anybody that needed to be "whooped." Most little boys go around talking like that. Though my dad was not extremely tall, he was extremely strong. He looked like he was carved out of stone. My dad always rolled up the sleeves of his auto body uniform, but he had to slit them first because his biceps bulged out of them, they were so big. There was one man who worked with him by the name of Herman. I'll never forget this precious man. Herman would say to my dad, "Mr. Jerry, you look like that man on the Arm & Hammer soda box." My dad actually had me convinced at one time that he posed for that picture.

**When God's people came up against something
they did not have the ability, the might
or the strength to deal with themselves,
the Strong One showed up.**

I feel the same way about my heavenly Father. My heavenly Father is the Strong One. Why should I fear when Satan comes against me? Why should I worry when attacks come into my life? Why should I give up when the Strong One is my Father?

More than Enough

God is also called the All-Sufficient One. That means that He's got plenty of whatever we may need in our lives. You are never going to find God running out of anything. There will not be a time when you ask Him to meet a financial need and He'll say that someone else prayed about 30 minutes before you and depleted heaven. God will never say He had to lay Jesus off, that the angels are on strike or that a depression has hit heaven and everyone is out of work. God is the All-Sufficient One. He can meet all our needs according to His riches in glory (see Phil. 4:19). It doesn't make any difference what the economy is doing down here; heaven's economy works under another system.

Many times, God has gone over and beyond when fulfilling my needs. There have been many times that He took care of me and I had plenty left over. Ephesians 3:20 tells us that God "is able to do exceeding abundantly above all that we ask or think" (*KJV*). There is no limit to His supply. How many Christians do you suppose there are on planet Earth right now? Do you know that if God met each of their needs and they had plenty left over, it wouldn't even dent His capital reserve? That's the God we serve.

Abraham's Experience of the Provider

Throughout the Bible, men and women who truly believed that God was the All-Sufficient One watched Him come through for them time and time again. They dared to believe that He would provide for them, and He never let them down. In Genesis we read the story of Abraham who was called by God to sacrifice his son Isaac.

> The next morning Abraham got up early. He saddled his donkey and took two of his servants with him, along with his son Isaac. Then he chopped wood to build a fire for a burnt offering and set out for the place where God had told him to go. On the third day of the journey, Abraham saw the place in the distance. "Stay here with the donkey," Abraham told the young men. "The boy and I will travel a little farther. We will worship there, and then we will come right back" (Gen. 22:3-5, *NLT*).

Abraham was a man of faith. Though he knew God was asking him to sacrifice his son, he told the servants, "You men stay here for a while. But don't worry, we'll be back." Abraham was so thoroughly convinced that God was his Provider that he said in faith that he and Isaac would return. He didn't know how God was going to do it, but he was sure that God would do it.

> Abraham placed the wood for the burnt offering on Isaac's shoulders, while he himself carried the knife and the fire. As the two of them went on together, Isaac said, "Father?" "Yes, my son," Abraham replied. "We have the wood and the fire," said the boy, "but where is the lamb for the sacrifice?" "*God will provide* a lamb, my son," Abraham answered. And they both went on together (Gen. 22:6-8, *NLT,* emphasis added).

No wonder the Bible tells us that we are to walk in the same steps of faith as our father Abraham. This man believed that God is. He believed that God would be everything he needed Him to be. And at that time, he needed God to be his provider. You see, a while back, God had made a promise to Abraham that a mighty nation would come from his son Isaac. Well, you can't get a nation out of a dead boy. So Abraham stood firm and "staggered not at the promise of God" (Rom. 4:20, *KJV*). He didn't hesitate to trust in God. He didn't question God's command to him. He had no reservations about taking that boy up on that mountain. Abraham was fully prepared if necessary to kill his son, burn his body to ashes and watch God raise those ashes up and resurrect Isaac, because of the promise God had given him.

When they arrived at the place where God had told Abraham to go, he built an altar and placed the wood on it. Then he tied Isaac up and laid him on the altar over the wood. And Abraham took the knife and lifted it up to kill his son as a sacrifice to the LORD. At that moment the angel of the LORD shouted to him from heaven, "Abraham! Abraham!" "Yes," he replied. "I'm listening." "Lay down the knife," the angel said. "Do not hurt the boy in any way, for now I know that you truly fear God. You have not withheld even your beloved son from me." Then Abraham looked up and saw a ram caught by its horns in a bush. So he took the ram and sacrificed it as a burnt offering on the altar in place of his son. Abraham named the place "The LORD Will Provide." This name has now become a proverb: "On the mountain of the LORD it will be provided" (Gen. 22:9-14, *NLT*).

The point of this story is that God, the Provider, showed up right in the nick of time. You may feel in your own life that God is late in meeting your need, but please understand that He is never late. God honored the promise He gave Abraham, and He honored Abraham's faith. Abraham said, "God will provide," and God provided a ram to be used as a sacrifice instead of Isaac. Abraham saw God demonstrate Himself as the Provider, and in honor of that, Abraham named that place Jehovah Jireh (God will provide). Every time Abraham passed by that place, it would remind him that his God was a providing God.

In the Old Testament it was not uncommon that when God manifested Himself in great battles and gave His children great victories, they would pile up stones in that spot as a memorial unto God. If I were to lay a stone in my front yard for every time God has come through for me in the last 40 years, you wouldn't even be able to see my house. But I do have memorials in my mind. I can remember every miracle, every breakthrough, every provision and every single time where God has come through for me.

Any time the devil says, "Jerry, you are not going to get your need met this time," I flip through a chart in my mind and think about the last time I had a need that looked impossible, and I remember how my Provider showed up. If He provided for me back then, then He'll do it again. Whatever you might be going through today, it's not too late for God to show up in your behalf. Don't ever give up on Him.

Another term in the Hebrew for Jehovah Jireh is "the Lord will see to it." I love that. It sounds like a guarantee, or a sure thing, to me. God is a sure thing. He is the surest thing in my life. I may not know about other people. I may not know what they are going to do, but I do know what my God is going to do. He is going to see to it that whatever He said will come to pass.

God proved to Abraham that if he dared to believe and dared to trust in Him, God would not allow His promises to fail in Abraham's life. I believe that God is saying the same thing to you and me. In the midst of every need we have, we should boldly declare, "My God will see to it. He will see to everything He has promised. He will see to it that it will come to pass just the way He said it."

The Supreme Being

I believe that is what John was referring to in Revelation 19:6 when he said, "For the Lord God omnipotent reigneth" (*KJV*). John described God as omnipotent, which means "possessing unlimited power and unlimited creative ability." What was John saying? That the God we serve possesses unlimited power. He possesses unlimited creative ability. Not only that, but He reigns. What does reign mean? It means that God has sovereign authority, supreme power and total dominion over everything in our lives.

Paul wrote about this omnipotent God who reigns:

Christ is the visible image of the invisible God. He existed before God made anything at all and is supreme over all creation. Christ is the one through whom God created everything in heaven and earth. He made the things we can see and the things we can't see—kings, kingdoms, rulers, and authorities. Everything has been created through him and for him. He existed before everything else began, and he holds all creation together. Christ is the head of the church, which is his body. He is the first of all who will rise from the dead, so he is first in everything (Col. 1:15-18, *NLT*).

Paul described a God to whom everything that has been created is subordinate to Him.

You might ask, "You mean He created evil?" "You mean He created sickness and disease?" "You mean He created poverty?"

No. God didn't create those things, but He did create Lucifer. And when Lucifer fell and God kicked him out of heaven, he came into Earth and began to bring about destruction and chaos. Lucifer created evil. Lucifer is the author of sickness and disease. He created poverty. But since God created Lucifer, then He says that HE will take full responsibility for him, and therefore no weapon formed against you shall prosper (see Isa. 54:17).

THE MESSAGE says that God is supreme. He was supreme in the beginning. He is supreme in the end. From the beginning to the end, He is there towering far above all of creation. Our God towers over every problem in our lives. How big is your financial need? How big is your marriage problem? How big is your health problem? Know that God towers over it and everything must bow to His awesome authority. God is greater than anything you are struggling with. God is greater than anything that looks impossible.

What is your need today? Are you weary? God is the rock in a weary land. Are you in the valley? God is the lily of the valley, the rose of Sharon, and the honey in the rock. Are you spiritually thirsty? God is the cup that runneth over. Are you comfortless? God is the rod and the staff that will comfort you. Are you lonely? God is a father to the orphan and a husband to the widow. Are you lost? God is the bright and morning star. He is the Almighty God. He is the everlasting God. He is the ever-present God. He is the all-powerful God. He is the most-high God. And thank God, He is the faithful God. He will be everything you need Him to be, if you'll dare believe it.

13

PURSUE, OVERTAKE AND RECOVER ALL

Are you tired of your situation? Are you tired of never being able to do the things that you want to do for your church, your family, your friends or your community? Are you tired of getting those past-due notices in the mail? Are you tired of never having anything in your savings account? Are you flat-out tired of struggling?

I reached that place more than 40 years ago. I was tired of always struggling. I was tired of all of my money going to somebody else. I didn't want to live like that anymore. Do you know what I did? I got fed up (I talked about this in great detail in chapter 4). I got angry about the bondage I was in. Once I got fed up, I took action, which eventually led to my turnaround. I'd like to share some principles with you about what action to take to pursue and overtake your Enemy and finally recover all that he has stolen from you.

Start Cheering Yourself On

King David in the Old Testament experienced a devastating plight when he came home from battle one time:

> Three days later, when David and his men arrived home at their town of Ziklag, they found that the Amalekites had made a raid into the Negev and had burned Ziklag to the ground. They had carried off the women and children and everyone else but without killing anyone. When David and his men saw the ruins and realized what had happened to their families, they wept until they could weep no more (1 Sam. 30:1-4, *NLT*).

David and his men had returned home from battle only to find their entire village burned to the ground. Their wives and children were taken captive. When they saw what had happened, they cried like babies. David was greatly distressed (see v. 6). Have you ever been greatly distressed? I have. I know what it's like to sit down and weep until there are no more tears to shed.

All of David's men began to blame him for this horror. They wanted to stone him and kill him. This was a pretty serious problem for David. At that moment, he had every reason or right to give up and quit. He could have said, "God, I'm a failure. I failed my men, and I have failed you." But that's not what happened. The Bible says, "David encouraged himself in the LORD" (1 Sam. 30:6, *KJV*). David became his own cheerleader. There wasn't anybody else to do it for him. Everyone else was either gone or they wanted him dead. David had to encourage himself. There may be times in your life when you will have to do the same thing. You're going to have to become your own best cheerleader.

**David had to encourage himself.
There may be times in your life when you will have
to do the same thing. You're going to have
to become your own best cheerleader.**

How did David encourage himself? He reminded himself of his covenant with the Almighty. And after spending time with God, David changed his attitude about his circumstance, and the strength of God entered into him. Instead of accepting defeat, the Bible says that he asked God, "Shall I pursue after this troop? Shall I overtake them?" God answered David, "Pursue: for thou shalt surely overtake them, and without fail recover all" (1 Sam. 30:8, *KJV*). That is what God wants you to do right now regarding your situation. He wants you to get fed up, encourage yourself in Him and then pursue, overtake and recover all.

How much longer are you going to put up with the devil stealing everything you've got? How much longer are you going to let him steal your finances, your peace and your freedom? How much longer are you going to tolerate him destroying your life? When are you going to take a stand for what rightfully belongs to you?

Just Say No to the Devil

I believe that it is time for you to become aggressive. It's time for you to take a stand for what rightfully belongs to you. You have a covenant right to all of the blessings of Abraham. The curse doesn't belong to you. Jesus took care of the curse at Calvary. Now it's time for you to enforce in your own life what Jesus has already provided for you.

"Be careful! Watch out for attacks from the Devil, your great enemy. He prowls around like a roaring lion, looking for some victim to devour. Take a firm stand against him, and be strong in your faith. Remember that your Christian brothers and sisters all over the world are going through the same kind of suffering you are" (1 Pet. 5:8-9, *NLT*). These verses tell us we don't have to accept whatever the devil is telling us. We don't have to buy into his lies. Peter told us to "take a firm stand against him, and be strong in [our] faith." Be aggressive. Start saying no to the devil. Stop entertaining the thoughts he throws your way. Start speaking the Word right in his face.

Let the devil know that you are fed up with bondage. Let him know that you are intolerant with lack. Let him know that you are through letting him steal from you. Let him know up front: "If it's a fight you want, it's a fight you're gonna get. But when the dust settles, God and I will be the ones still standing!"

You can't be passive. You can't sit back and hope that someday your situation will turn around. You can't believe that if it's the will of God for you to live in divine prosperity, then it will just happen without your believing for it. You'll be broke the rest of your life if you keep thinking like that. You could lose everything.

Take a bold and energetic stand. It's time to be militant about what belongs to you. Being militant implies a vigorous, unrelenting pursuit. Get militant toward the enemy. Get confident and have a persistent determination to express what you believe. What do you believe? You believe the Word and you believe that "greater is He that is in you, than he that is in the world" (1 John 4:4, *KJV*).

You've got to keep what you believe front and center in the devil's face every day. Wake up every morning telling him that he is not going to devour you. Then, like a machine gun, start rapid firing the Word out of your mouth. Don't even give him a chance to start on you first. You've got to become more persistent than he is.

You might be thinking, *Yeah, but, brother Jerry, the devil just won't leave me alone.* Your thoughts are silenced when you speak words out of your mouth. You can't combat your thoughts with thoughts. You have to use the Word of God. When you are constantly speaking the Word over your life, then those bad thoughts have to eventually become quiet. And ultimately, your thoughts will line up with the Word.

Peter also pointed out that you are not the only one going through these attacks. "Remember that your Christian brothers and sisters all over the world are going through the same kind of suffering you are" (1 Pet. 5:9). You are not the only one facing financial difficulties. You are not the only one facing health problems. You are not the only one going through whatever it is that you're going through. Others have gone through it and some folks are going through it right now. So don't throw a pity party for yourself. Don't walk around with the attitude, "Nobody knows the trouble I've seen . . . nobody knows my sorrow." That's a lie. Instead of wasting your energy on feeling sorry for yourself, get fed up and begin to do something about it.

Keep Standing

"A final word: Be strong with the Lord's mighty power. Put on all of God's armor so that you will be able to stand firm against all strategies and tricks of the Devil. For we are not fighting against people made of flesh and blood, but against the evil rulers and authorities of the unseen world, against those mighty powers of darkness who rule this world, and against wicked spirits in the heavenly realms. Use every piece of God's armor to resist the enemy in the time of evil, so that after the battle you will still be standing firm" (Eph. 6:10-13, *NLT*).

After you've done everything, then you must stand firm. Standing firm leaves no room for compromise. Anything less than standing firm is to yield to the enemy. Anything less than standing firm is to doubt God's ability to deliver you.

**Standing firm leaves no room for compromise.
Anything less than standing firm is to yield to the enemy
and doubt God's ability to deliver you.**

Rejoice!

I remember one time when I was in a situation where I had stood for a long time, and I didn't feel like I could stand any longer. I felt like my spiritual armor was falling apart. My helmet was falling off. My breastplate was barely hanging on. It seemed as though I had so many fiery darts in my shield of faith that there wasn't any room for one more.

I asked God, "What do I do next?" His answer to me was, "Rejoice, because you have the devil exactly where you want him." I asked Him if I could get a second opinion about the matter. After all, I could barely keep standing as it was. God kept repeating, "Rejoice. Rejoice. Rejoice." Finally He said, "Son, you may not feel as strong as you did when you first started this endeavor, but there's one thing you can say right now. Even though you may be shaky, even though you may feel like your armor is falling off, take a good look at yourself. You're still standing!"

If you are under the greatest pressure that you have ever been under, that's a good indication that you've got the devil right where you want him. I want to suggest to you what God suggested to me: *rejoice!*

Get on the Offense

Instead of being in a defensive mode, it's time to get on the offensive. It's time to get your sword out and start swinging! It's time to get in the devil's face and say, "Now listen to me. I am prepared for battle. I am ready. God is on my side. And if God is on my side, who can be against me? Furthermore, no weapon formed against me shall prosper! I'm called to battle, and I am destined to win!"

Let the Hand of God Work for You

Over and over throughout the Bible, we see the phrases "the hand of the Lord" or "the hand of God." When you read these words it always represents two things: (1) God's power expressed in judgment, and (2) God's power expressed in blessing. When the hand of the Lord is involved, then there is always judgment for the adversary and blessing for God's people. Here are some illustrations.

> So I will reach out and strike at the heart of Egypt with all kinds of miracles. Then at last he will let you go. And I will see to it that the Egyptians treat you well. They will load you down with gifts so you will not leave empty-handed (Exod. 3:20-21, *NLT*).

In the context of this Scripture, the nation of Israel had been in captivity under Egyptian rule for about 400 years, and God was creating a plan for their deliverance. Notice that this passage speaks about judgment (God will strike the Egyptians), and also about blessing (God will cause the Egyptians to look favorably upon the Israelites). What happened? God's people left the land of slavery with all the treasure of Egypt. They left with more than they had come into captivity with.

> Now they which were scattered abroad upon the persecution that arose about Stephen travelled as far as Phenice, and Cyprus, and Antioch, preaching the word to none but unto the Jews only. And some of them were men of Cyprus and Cyrene, which, when they were come to Antioch, spake unto the Grecians, preaching the Lord Jesus. And the hand of the Lord was with them: and a great number believed, and turned unto the Lord (Acts 11:19-21, *KJV*).

Paul was writing in Acts about how the early church was being persecuted. The eleventh chapter of Acts speaks of how God made the devil pay for this persecution by adding souls to the church in multitudes. The blessing for the church was that a great number of believers came into the kingdom of God. The devil lost souls and God gained souls. When the hand of the Lord is manifested, Satan will be penalized and God's people will be compensated.

> "And now, O Lord, hear their threats, and give your servants great boldness in their preaching. Send your healing power; may miraculous signs and wonders be done

through the name of your holy servant Jesus." After this prayer, the building where they were meeting shook, and they were all filled with the Holy Spirit. And they preached God's message with boldness. All the believers were of one heart and mind, and they felt that what they owned was not their own; they shared everything they had. And the apostles gave a powerful witness to the resurrection of the Lord Jesus, and God's great favor was upon them all (Acts 4:29-33, *NLT*).

This portion of Scripture shows us that the early church prayed that God would stretch forth His hand, and the Lord responded. He gave them His power, and more souls came into the Kingdom.

**Take your burdens out of your hands
and put them in God's hands. If you get a revelation
of the mighty hand of God and humble yourself before Him,
you will see Him move on your behalf.**

God wants us to let Him work on our behalf. In the Scripture, He even asks us to give Him a mandate to carry out for us. Isaiah 45:11 says, "Concerning the work of my hands command ye me" (*KJV*). *Strong's Exhaustive Concordance* states that the word "command," as it is used in this passage, means "to appoint." The word "appoint" means "to assign" or "to commission." What God is saying here is, "Give Me an assignment. Commission Me to do something on your behalf." If you let Him work on your behalf, He will bring judgment on the adversary and make him pay damages for what he has put you through; and He will bless you.

Peter gave us the reminder to humble ourselves under the hand of God (see 1 Pet. 5:6). Why? So that God can exalt us in due time. Peter went on to say that we should do this especially when we are going through an impossible-looking situation that has burdened us with its care. He offered, "Give all your worries and cares to God, for he cares about what happens to you" (1 Pet. 5:7, *NLT*). This literally means to take your burdens out of your hands and put them in God's hands. His hands are more capable than your hands anyway. If you get a revelation of the mighty hand of God and humble yourself before Him, you will see Him move on your behalf.

Make Satan Pay

It's time for you to pursue your adversary. It's time for you to overtake him. It's time for you to storm the gates of hell and demand that he pay back everything that he has stolen from you.

Just think about all those times when unexpected things happened—things you weren't planning on happening. Remember the trip to the emergency room for your child who got sick in the middle of the night? What was that? That was an attack from the enemy sent to steal from you. What about when you went out one morning and discovered that your car wouldn't start? It had been running fine the day before. What was that? That was an attack from the enemy sent to steal from you. Just think about all the things the devil has attacked you with. Think about how much money he has robbed you of. Think about all the joy he has stolen from you. Doesn't that make you mad? It should.

Would you let a thief come into your house and steal everything you owned without a fight? I wouldn't (and I sure hope you wouldn't). We wouldn't tell the burglar, "Oh yes, you can have whatever you want. Take everything. It doesn't matter to me. I really don't need it." No. That thief would have a fight on his hands. Yet that is what the devil has been doing to the Body of Christ for years. He comes in, steals from us and we let him have our stuff. We don't even put up a fight for what is rightfully ours. It's time that changed.

Some years ago, God woke me up in the middle of the night and began to speak to me. He said, "My people are letting their adversary get away with too much, and they are not making him pay for what he has put them through. They are letting him off too lightly! Don't just pray for deliverance from the attacks, but commission Me to bring judgment on the one who attacks you."

"Men do not despise a thief, if he steal to satisfy his soul when he is hungry; but if he be found, he shall restore *sevenfold*; he shall give all the substance of his house" (Prov. 6:30-31, *KJV*, emphasis added). Notice that God says if you catch a thief, don't just revel in the fact that you caught him—make him pay for damages sevenfold!

Satan is a thief. He has been let off too easy. By your commissioning God to bring judgment upon him, Satan is forced to not only stop his attack, but to also pay for all the damage he has caused in your life. Whatever his attacks have cost you, God wants him to pay it back, and not less than sevenfold.

So stop praying just for deliverance. Begin to ask God to make the devil pay for what he has done to you. It's time for you to call on the hand of God. Don't you want the devil to suffer for what he has done to you? All those sleepless nights, the mental anguish, the loss of finances, the headaches, the bundles of stress. Get on the offensive, declare war on bondage and lack, and call on the hand of God.

God's will is for you to be the victor in every battle you fight. But you must become aggressive. Don't be passive any longer. Get on the offensive, start calling on the hand of God and watch your situation turn around for the good. If you'll refuse to quit, if you'll refuse to give up and will stand firm, there is nothing the devil can do to defeat you. The Holy Spirit will supply you with the power to pursue, overtake and recover all that the devil has stolen from you.

14

SHOUT IT OUT

The Journey of Faith and Shipwrecks

Nobody wants to start out in a boat and end up shipwrecked. When you set out in a boat, you expect to reach your destination safely, and you expect to get back from where you started safely. Nobody in his or her right mind gets out on the boat hoping to become shipwrecked and not make it back home.

The same concept applies to the walk of faith. I want to teach you in this chapter how to avoid what I call a shipwreck in your journey of faith. You shouldn't expect to be defeated. You shouldn't expect to win a few, lose a few. You should expect to win them all. We are partakers of God's divine nature and, as best as I can tell, God is a winner. So God made us to win.

Living here on Earth can be good if you know how to do it God's way. I'm not in any big hurry to get to heaven. I'm going to get there eventually, but I'm not in any rush. I'm learning how to take God's Word and apply it to my circumstances down here and live a victorious life. Jesus prayed to the Father, "May your will be done here on earth, just as it is in heaven" (Matt. 6:10, *NLT*). You can actually have some of heaven right down here!

We all have opportunities for sickness. Opportunities for failure. Opportunities for lack. Opportunities for grief and sorrow. Opportunities to give up. But you don't have to accept these opportunities. All you have to do is say, "No thank you, devil, I'm free from all of that in Jesus' Name!"

In the book of 1 Timothy, Paul wrote to a young minister named Timothy. He told this young man, "Timothy, my son, here are my instructions for you, based on the prophetic words spoken about you earlier. May they give you the confidence to fight well in the Lord's battles. Cling tightly to your faith in Christ, and always keep your conscience clear. For some people have deliberately violated their consciences; as a result, their faith has been shipwrecked" (1 Tim. 1:18-19, *NLT*).

Notice that those who did not hold on to their faith ended up shipwrecked. Getting shipwrecked doesn't sound much like success, does it? If you end up shipwrecked, it sounds like you were defeated. God never intends for that to happen. He wants you to come out on the other side a winner, and He wants you to come out better equipped for the next faith endeavor. Paul said that living by faith is akin to running a race. It's not a 100-yard dash though; it's more like a cross-country endurance race. When I was in high school, I used to run the mile, and boy, I'll never forget how they trained us. You didn't just give it everything you had for a short distance. No, you paced yourself. You knew that you had a long way to go and you wanted to finish strong. It's the same in the life of faith.

The Problem with Being Discouraged

"And they journeyed from mount Hor by the way of the Red sea, to compass the land of Edom: and the soul of the people was *much discouraged* because of the way" (Num. 21:4, *KJV*, emphasis added). The people of Israel were involved in a faith journey. They had been delivered out of bondage in Egypt and were now headed for the Promised Land. The Bible tells us they were "much discouraged because of the way."

Let me tell you something about discouragement. How many times have you read in the Bible the words "Be of good courage"? Discouragement is the opposite of that. In fact, God told Joshua to not be discouraged four times after he took the place of Moses in leading Israel. To be of good courage means "the attitude, response or ability to face and deal bravely and fearlessly with anything recognized as being difficult, painful and even dangerous without withdrawing from it."

In every situation put before you, God wants you to stand fearlessly and without withdrawing from it. That's the reason He told us to resist the devil.

Many times you hear of courage described by what people do in dangerous situations. That's how God wants His people to be. In every situation put before you that could prove difficult or even be dangerous, God wants you to stand fearlessly and without withdrawing from it. That's the reason He told us to resist the devil. He didn't say that when we experience great difficulty we are to run like the wind.

In Ephesians 6:10-18, Paul talks about the spiritual armor that God wants us to put on. Notice that it's all worn on the front of the body. There is no weapon for the backside because we're not in the business of retreating. It's about moving forward. Paul never mentions backing off. He never mentions taking on the attitude of a coward.

Being discouraged also means having a lack of confidence. Have you ever gone along real well in your journey of faith, confessing the Word and being full of joy, and then a bad report comes your way? There's a tendency to pay close attention to it. If you start dwelling on that bad report, it will drop down into your spirit, and then your confidence in God will be lost.

The people of Israel became so discouraged because they took their eyes off of what God had said. They focused their attention on their circumstances, and all it produced was discouragement. The first thing that happens when you get discouraged is that you start doubting God. When you doubt God, then you doubt His Word. You say things that are contrary to what God says. When you're discouraged, you stop saying, "The joy of the Lord is my strength and I can do all things through Christ who strengthens me." When you are discouraged, you talk what the devil says; and when this happens, then you are headed for a shipwreck.

Discouragement is a destroyer of faith. Psalm 31 tells what happens when you start doubting God. "For I said in my haste, I am cut off from before thine eyes" (Ps. 31:22, *KJV*). In their discouragement, a lot of people say things like this: "I don't know why God never answers my prayers." Don't allow yourself to talk like that. Cast those thoughts down and speak what God says. He says that He will never forsake you.

Let's read what the writer of this psalm later says: "O, love the LORD all ye his saints: for the LORD preserveth the faithful, and plentifully rewardeth the proud doer. Be of good courage, and he shall strengthen your heart, all ye that hope in the LORD"

(Ps. 31:23-24, *KJV*). We need to hope in the Lord and refuse to become discouraged. God rewards those who remain confident.

I know the feeling of discouragement very well. I got so mad at brother Kenneth Copeland one time in the early days of my Christianity. It wasn't his fault, of course. I was the one who wasn't doing things right. For hours, every day, I would listen to his tapes over and over and over and over again. Night and day, day and night, I listened to them and nothing seemed to be changing my situation. Brother Copeland came to my town one night and I asked him what my problem was. He said, "It's your big mouth."

That made me so mad. If he only knew the time I had spent listening to him on tapes. Well, I went home, grabbed one of his tapes and threw it down the street. In my anger and in my haste, I threw out the very answer to my problem. As I watched it roll down the road, I quickly thought, *Dear God, there goes my answer.* So what did I do? I ran down the street, picked it up and took it back home and played it again. Eventually, things started changing around my house.

Start Making Good Confessions

Job had this same problem once. Did you know that God revealed to him that his problem was his mouth? "Did I say, Bring unto me? or, Give a reward for me of your substance? Or, Deliver me from the enemy's hand'? or, Redeem me from the hand of the mighty? Teach me, and I will hold my tongue: and cause me to understand wherein I have erred" (Job 6:22-24, *KJV*). In other words, Job told God, "I've been wrong, Lord, but if you teach me,

I will shut my mouth." Then Job made this powerful statement: "How forcible are right words!" (Job 6:25, *KJV*).

Job got a revelation of the power of words. He got a revelation of how powerful his words really were. He realized that he was in error through the words of his mouth. I touched on this matter in chapter 8, but I want to explore it in greater detail. Did you know that when you have fear, you talk fear; and when you have faith, you talk faith? Fear and faith are released by both words and actions.

When you have fear, you talk fear; and when you have faith, you talk faith. Fear and faith are released by both words and actions.

When Job said earlier, "For the thing which I greatly feared is come upon me" (Job 3:25, *KJV*), he was talking his fear, and God finally pointed out that his problem was his mouth. You would think that once Job learned this he would take control of his tongue, right? If you found out today that all of the tragedy in your life came about through the words of your mouth, would you do something about your words? Would you be smart enough to correct it?

The Bible teaches, "For whatever is in your heart determines what you say" (Matt. 12:34, *NLT*). Bad things come out of your mouth as a result of what is in your heart in the same way that good things come out as a result of what is in your heart. Job found out his mouth was getting him in trouble. Unfortunately, he didn't do a very good job with this revelation. Read what he said just a little while later.

> Is this not the struggle of all humanity? A person's life is long and hard, like that of a hired hand, like a worker who longs for the day to end, like a servant waiting to be paid. I, too, have been assigned months of futility, long and weary nights of misery. When I go to bed, I think, "When will it be morning?" But the night drags on, and I toss till dawn. My skin is filled with worms and scabs. My flesh breaks open, full of pus. My days are swifter than a weaver's shuttle flying back and forth. They end without hope. O God, remember that my life is but a breath, and I will never again experience pleasure. You see me now, but not for long. Your eyes will be on me, but I will be dead. Just as a cloud dissipates and vanishes, those who die will not come back. They are gone forever from their home—never to be seen again. "I cannot keep from speaking. I must express my anguish. I must complain in my bitterness" (Job 7:1-11, *NLT*).

The man had just found out that his mouth was getting him in trouble, but he got discouraged again and said, "I don't care. I am not going to hold my tongue." I would say that Job got "much discouraged," wouldn't you?

Perhaps you have received a revelation of the power of the words of your mouth. You realize how creative and destructive the tongue is and how forcible right words are. You make every effort to say the right things. But the minute adversity comes, you have an opportunity to do what Job did. You have an opportunity to speak in your haste. You have an opportunity to speak against the Word. And if you do, then you put yourself on the path to getting shipwrecked.

We have played around long enough with whether this confession teaching is right or wrong. The Bible declares it and it's time that we accept it. The truth is, according to numerous Scriptures in the Bible, your words will make you or break you. Therefore, you need to take control of them or they will destroy you.

It's Time to Start Shouting

Job got discouraged. He said, "I know words are forceful. I know how I have been wrong with my mouth. But I don't care. I'm hurting. I've got problems, and I am not shutting up." This was a mistake; and had he not later corrected it, then it could have made matters worse.

The Lord shared something with me one day that really blessed me. It's not too often that He talks to me when I'm watching TV, but I saw this commercial about a laundry detergent called "Shout," which is designed to remove all kinds of spots and stains. I'm sure you've heard of it or have even seen the commercial. In this television advertisement, a little boy is playing and splashing around in the mud when a voice in the background speaks to the mother watching this boy: "What are you going to do about this mud stain?" The mother replies, "I'm going to Shout it out!" Then a little girl who is jumping rope gets a lot of grime all over her clothes and the same voice asks, "What are you going to do about your daughter's dress?" The mother comes back with the same answer: "I am going to Shout it out!"

As I was watching that commercial, the Lord asked me, "Jerry, what are you going to do when you get discouraged?" (Bingo!) I said, "I am going to shout it out!" And I've been shouting it out ever since.

The New Testament records the words "Be of good cheer" many times. Jesus even said it. "Be of good cheer; it is I; be not afraid" (Matt. 14:27, *KJV*). Think about the words "good cheer." Have you ever heard of a bad cheer? Have you ever gone to a football game and heard the cheerleaders yell, "Gimmie me a 'D,' gimmie an 'E,' gimmie an 'F,' gimmie me an 'E,' gimmie an 'A,' gimmie a 'T.' What's that spell? Defeat! Defeat! Defeat!" Of course not. Let me tell you what "be of good cheer" means. Cheer is encouragement, being full of joy, being excited and in good spirits. It's also defined as a shout.

When discouragement tries to set in on you, just shout it out! You can't shout the praises of God and stay discouraged at the same time.

So how do you avoid a shipwreck during your journey of faith? When discouragement tries to set in on you, just *shout it out!* There are times when I'm driving on the freeway in my car and the devil starts whispering in my ears, "You are not going to build this and you are not going to build that. This isn't going to work and that isn't going to work." What do I do? I shout it out. I shout out my V-I-C-T-O-R-Y. It's time to start shouting it out. You can't shout the praises of God and stay discouraged at the same time.

God knew about this "shout it out" stuff way before the laundry detergent makers did. Why do you think the Scriptures tell us when God's people were outnumbered in battle that God commanded the praise and worship singers to stand on the front line? He wanted them to shout out at the enemy!

Early the next morning the army of Judah went out into the wilderness of Tekoa. On the way Jehoshaphat stopped and said, "Listen to me, all you people of Judah and Jerusalem! Believe in the LORD your God, and you will be able to stand firm. Believe in his prophets, and you will succeed." After consulting the leaders of the people, *the king appointed singers to walk ahead of the army, singing to the LORD and praising him for his holy splendor. This is what they sang: "Give thanks to the LORD; his faithful love endures forever!"* At the moment they began to sing and give praise, the LORD caused the armies of Ammon, Moab, and Mount Seir to start fighting among themselves. The armies of Moab and Ammon turned against their allies from Mount Seir and killed every one of them. After they had finished off the army of Seir, they turned on each other. So when the army of Judah arrived at the lookout point in the wilderness, there were dead bodies lying on the ground as far as they could see. Not a single one of the enemy had escaped (2 Chron. 20:20-24, *NLT*).

These people shouted out praises unto the Lord and it blew the enemy's game plan. The enemy turned on one another and killed themselves. Do you want to know what happened next? The people of Israel went out in victory carrying all of their enemies' spoils. The Bible says it was even "more than they could carry. There was so much plunder that it took them three days just to collect it all" (2 Chron. 20:25, *NLT*).

You need to become your own cheerleader. You can do this in your home. When one of your family members gets depressed, jump up and say, "Let's get in the Word. C'mon! Let's get in the Word! Our God will supply all our needs! It's not over yet! C'mon! Hallelujah! Shout it out! Praise the Lord!"

There is much power in the name of Jesus. He is far above principalities, power, might, dominion and every name that is named. The name of Jesus is so powerful that the Bible calls Him the Word of God. When you speak His name, you have just thrown at the devil, all at one time, Genesis to Revelation. We need to shout out the name of Jesus and spoil the devil's day. We need to let him know that we are not pushovers. We need to remind him that he is up against a winning team. We need to let him know he is going to lose.

"Clap your hands, all ye people; shout unto God with the voice of triumph" (Ps. 47:1, *KJV*). Start shouting to God with a triumphant voice. If you've got financial problems, shout out your prosperity. If you've got health problems, shout out your healing. If you've got work issues, shout out your victory. If you're discouraged, shout out your joy! Remember, God created you to be a champion. He made you to be a winner. You have been called to battle, but you *are destined to win!*

Further Resources

For additional products, including books, audios and videos,
visit the Jerry Savelle Ministries Int'l. website at

WWW.JERRYSAVELLE.ORG

USA Office
Jerry Savelle Ministries, Int'l.
P.O. Box 748
Crowley, TX 76036-3155
Phone: 817-297-3155

Australia Office
Jerry Savelle Ministries, Int'l.
Australia Office
Locked Bag 200
Gold Coast Mail Center
Bundall, 9726 QLD, Australia
61 7 5526-6522

Canada Office
Jerry Savelle Ministries Int'l.
P.O. Box 7000
Lambeth Station
London, Ontario
N6P 1W4
519-652-1611

Europe Office
Jerry Savelle Ministries, Int'l.
School Hill Centre
Chepstow
Monmouthshire
NP16 5PH UK
44(0) 1291 628071